8.99

Social
aviour

This book describes the nature and causes of pro-social and anti-social behaviour. It is an introductory level text aimed at students new to this area of Social Psychology. Topics covered include social psychological theories of aggression, altruism and bystander behaviour, and media influences on pro-social and anti-social behaviour. Each section includes information on research carried out in these areas of study.

David Clarke teaches A level psychology and is an A level examiner. Since 1993 he has been a principal examiner for the OCR examining board.

Routledge Modular Psychology

Series editors: Cara Flanagan is a Reviser for AS and A2 level Psychology and an experienced teacher and examiner. Philip Banyard is Associate Senior Lecturer in Psychology at Nottingham Trent University and a Chief Examiner for AS and A2 level Psychology. Both are experienced writers.

The *Routledge Modular Psychology* series is a completely new approach to introductory-level psychology, tailor-made to the new modular style of teaching. Each short book covers a topic in more detail than any large textbook can, allowing teacher and student to select material exactly to suit any particular course or project.

The books have been written especially for those students new to higher-level study, whether at school, college or university. They include specially designed features to help with technique, such as a model essay at an average level with an examiners comments to show how extra marks can be gained. The authors are all examiners and teachers at the introductory level.

The *Routledge Modular Psychology* texts are all user-friendly and accessible and use the following features:

- practice essays with specialist commentary to show how to achieve a higher grade
- chapter summaries to assist with revision
- progress and review exercises
- glossary of key terms
- summaries of key research
- further reading to stimulate ongoing study and research
- cross-referencing to other books in the series

For more details on our AS, A2 and *Routledge Modular Psychology* publications visit our website at www.a-levelpsychology.co.uk

Also available in this series (titles listed by syllabus section):

To Victoria, Rachael and James without whose help this book, and most other things in my life, would have been impossible to achieve.

Pro-Social and Anti-Social Behaviour

David Clarke

Routledge
Taylor & Francis Group

LONDON AND NEW YORK

First published 2003
by Routledge
27 Church Road, Hove, East Sussex BN3 2FA

Simultaneously published in the USA and Canada
by Routledge
29 West 35th Street, New York NY 10001

Routledge is an imprint of the Taylor & Francis Group

Typeset in Times and Frutiger by Keystroke,
Jacaranda Lodge, Wolverhampton
Printed and bound in Great Britain by
TJ International Ltd, Padstow, Cornwall
Paperback cover design by Anú Design

British Library Cataloguing in Publication Data
A catalogue record for this book is available from the British Library

Library of Congress Cataloging-in-Publication Data
Clarke, David, 1958–
  Pro-social and anti-social behaviour / David Clarke.
     p. cm. — (Routledge modular psychology)
  Includes bibliographical references and index.
  ISBN 0-415-22760-7 (hbk) — ISBN 0-415-22761-5 (pbk.)
   1. Interpersonal relations. 2. Interpersonal conflict. 3. Social
  psychology. 4. Human behavior. I. Title. II. Series.
  HM1106.C49 2003
  302—dc21

                              2003000279

                    ISBN 0–415–22760–7 (hbk)
                    ISBN 0–415–22761–5 (pbk)

Contents

Illustrations

Figures

Tables

Acknowledgements

The series editors and Routledge acknowledge the expert help of Paul Humphreys, Examiner and Reviser for AS and A2 level Psychology, in compiling the Study aids chapter of each book in the series.

AQA (AEB) examination questions are reproduced by permission of the Assessment and Qualifications Alliance. The AQA do not accept any responsibility for the answers or examiner comments in the Study aids chapter of this book or any other in the series.

The author would also like to thank Brenda Clarke for her lifelong support, Victoria Clarke for not writing her book first, James Clarke for making cups of tea, Rachael Clarke for not making cups of tea and Beth Black for her invaluable contributions to the writing of this book.

Introducing pro- and anti-social behaviour

Introducing pro-social behaviour
Introducing anti-social behaviour
Psychological approaches to pro-social behaviour
Psychological approaches to anti-social behaviour

Have you ever wondered why people go out of their way to watch when someone is hurt or injured? Consider the following instances. We often see car drivers slow down their cars to see what has happened in the accident on the opposite carriageway. Why do people behave in this way? This fascination may be explained by us not wanting to see one of our species injured and we are concerned to see that they will survive. But look at it another way. Why is it when two children fight in a school playground we see a huddle of other children immediately form around them, desperate to watch? Is this because they want to see if one survives the ordeal? I think not. It is much more likely that they want to see one child getting injured in some way, to know which child is dominant. We watch a strange mixture of television programmes too. Real-life situations where people have survived against the odds have become very popular recently but then we also watch violent films and sports involving aggressive behaviour.

A number of social-psychological theories have been proposed which suggest that the society in which we live and the features of modern life *determine* our behaviours. Another explanation proposes that behaviour results from an interaction of physiological arousal (e.g. how alert/emotional we are) and cognitive processing (e.g. how we assess a situation). There are some psychologists who believe that our propensity to behave in a pro- or anti-social way is inherited (part of our genetic make-up), and yet others believe we learn all our behaviour, whether pro- or anti-social, from parents and significant others. An important consideration is the extent to which the media influence our behaviour. A number of studies have shown that exposure to television violence is positively correlated with violent behaviour. Other studies suggest the relationship is weak and that viewers do discriminate between real life and fictional violence. It is also argued by some that television can be used to reduce aggressive behaviour and encourage pro-social behaviour.

Introducing pro-social behaviour

We have all probably helped other people at some time in our lives and most of us help others many times each day. Our giving of help need not be complex; it may be nothing more than holding a door open for someone loaded with books or shopping or a parent carrying a child. We may also help the proverbial old lady to cross the road. For situations like this we can define helping simply as the giving of assistance to another person. Helping is one facet of **pro-social behaviour** which Batson (1998: 282) believes is 'the broad range of actions intended to benefit one or more people other than oneself – behaviours such as helping, comforting, sharing and co-operation.'

If we can explain helping and pro-social behaviour so easily, why are psychologists interested in studying it? Well, let me ask you a question. Why do some people fail to give assistance, such as helping the old lady to cross the road?

You might explain this difference by saying that some people have more time to spare than others do. However, consider that if someone does not help the old lady she may well become injured as she attempts to cross the busy road. Surely someone could now spare the time to help her?

Real-life examples

Now let me take your kindness a step further and ask you the question: what about a life or death situation: would you risk your life to save someone else? Your answer, which may well be that 'it depends', is what has fascinated psychologists and this is why they study pro-social behaviour.

History has revealed numerous spectacular examples where heroes have sacrificed their own lives to save the lives of others. Consider the rescuers of Jews in Nazi Europe such as Miep Gies who helped hide Anne Frank and her family and Oskar Schindler who saved the lives of thousands. On 24 October 1999 Frank Foley, 'the British Schindler', was awarded Israel's highest honour for a non-Jew for saving 10,000 people from the Holocaust. Why did these people risk their own safety for others – many of whom were strangers to them?

There are also cases where people involved in technological catastrophes have saved others. On 13 January 1982, Air Florida Flight 90, taking off from Washington DC, hit a bridge and plunged into the icy waters of the Potomac River. America later applauded the selfless acts of two men. The first was Lenny Skutnik, a passer-by, who stopped and watched as rescuers tried to pull survivors out of the river. When Priscilla Tirado lost her grip on a helicopter lifeline and started to sink, of all those witnessing the events only Skutnik, who later explained, 'Somebody had to go into the water', risked his own life by jumping into the water and pulling her to safety. The second man, Arland Williams (a passenger on the flight), continuously passed the rope from the rescue helicopter to other passengers. When the helicopter returned for him, he was nowhere to be found.

Animals have even been known to help people. In 1996 Binti Tua, a gorilla at Brookfield Zoo, Chicago, kept other gorillas away and then picked up and placed a 3-year-old boy, who had fallen into the gorilla pit, at the zookeeper's door from where he could be rescued.

Why help others?

In the above examples some of the heroes survived but some did not. It may be the case that as the situation developed before their eyes they assessed the situation, decided they could survive the event and so helped because of the glory they would receive. Quite clearly we do honour the courageousness of their behaviour. But what about those who did not survive? Perhaps they expected to survive and receive the glory but their unfortunate miscalculation of events resulted in their deaths. However, when such surviving heroes are questioned about the motivation for their actions a frequent response is that ' I didn't have time to think'. And, if we were to stop and think we would probably still be standing there long after everyone else had gone home! So the motivation can't be for the possible rewards.

Would you risk your life to save others? Perhaps you would but many people would not. It depends, of course, on who needs help. Suppose your house is on fire and your daughters are trapped inside. Would you hesitate? David Veivers faced precisely this situation in February 2000 and did not hesitate. After rescuing his wife, eldest daughter and two other girls he returned for his two younger daughters. Unable to survive what was described as an inferno he and his daughters lost their lives.

So would you risk your life to save others who are strangers to you? For Lenny Skutnik the answer was clearly yes but in this case there was no apparent danger. A major factor that determines whether people help or not is whether helping would put themselves in danger and if that danger is apparent they are less likely to help. Consider the following examples.

Shortly after Christmas in 1981, while postwoman Karen Green was at work delivering mail in Arizona she was assaulted by three men and two women, all of whom were drunk. As she struggled for fifteen minutes with her attackers, people witnessing the situation telephoned the police several times but did not directly intervene. Finally, she was forced into a car and driven away. Her body was found two days later. No one helped, possibly because they feared that they too might have been harmed.

In Manhattan, New York in 1982 a woman was being attacked in a car park by a man, and three CBS technicians passing by decided to help her. For their trouble, all three were shot and killed by the attacker.

The Kitty Genovese tragedy

If people don't directly intervene at very least they could telephone for help as in the case of Karen Green above. In some cases they do not even do that. In 1964, New Yorker Catherine 'Kitty' Genovese,

28, was returning home at 3 a.m. from her work as a bar manager. As she neared home, which was in a middle-class neighbourhood of the New York borough of Queens, Winston Moseley jumped out of the shadows and attacked her. She screamed as loudly as she could, 'Oh my God, he stabbed me! Please help me! Please help me!' (Rosenthal 1964: 33) and tried to defend herself. Her attacker was frightened away twice by lights coming on in windows, but he returned each time and his third attack, as Miss Genovese tried to crawl into an apartment block, was fatal. Police later discovered that although 38 people heard her screams and many looked out of their windows and saw the attack, no one went to her rescue and no one picked up a telephone to call the police until after she was dead. (Moseley, convict No. 64A0102, is currently in Great Meadow State Prison, New York State.)

It seems that the witnesses considered the situation and decided that if they intervened it might well result in harm to themselves: they could be injured or even killed. All thirty-eight observers may have decided that they did not want to be heroes or come to harm. So why did no one pick up the telephone? Surely this simple act might have saved Kitty's life without any risk to themselves whatsoever. A twist to this story is that many people believed the Genovese family was involved with the Mafia and so feared reprisals if they intervened.

Defining pro-social behaviour

The crucial question, after considering more real-life examples, is why do some people behave pro-socially when others do not? We have already considered several possible answers and yet another possible answer to this question is that it revolves around two motives: egoism and altruism. The first, **egoism**, is when we are motivated by self-interest: we help because it makes us feel good. Those advocating this view believe that self-benefit is always the ultimate goal of helping. Alternatively, the second motive, **altruism**, is where we help to benefit another rather than to benefit ourselves. As an act altruism has two properties: it must benefit someone else and it must be potentially costly to the benefactor. More formally, Walster and Piliavin (1972) define altruism as, 'helping behaviour that is voluntary, costly to the altruist and motivated by something other than the expectation of material or social reward'. This definition makes the distinction between egoism and altruism clear because there is a regard for the interest of others without apparent concern for one's self-interest or obvious external rewards.

If egoism is our motivation then we help when we want the glory our actions will receive and we do not help when it is safer for us not to do so. At all times our concern is for ourselves. Anticipation of a delayed reward is often the hidden motive for a great deal of what is claimed to be altruistic behaviour. Many countries offer official rewards for services to the community but more often than not these services have been undertaken not for altruistic reasons but in the anticipation that they are award worthy. Simply, very few public honours come as a surprise.

If we help because of altruism the furthest thing from our minds is glory or what may happen to us. The definition provided by Walster and Piliavin, using the words 'motivated by something other than', is good because it states simply that psychologists are still interested in altruistic behaviour because we want to know just exactly what that something is.

Although McDougal first asked the question in the early 1900s as to why people do – and don't – behave pro-socially, it was only in the 1960s, with the occurrence of a number of events such as the murder of Kitty Genovese, that psychologists began to focus their attention. It is estimated that in the 20 years between 1962 and 1982 over 1,000 academic articles on helping behaviour and altruism had been published, establishing it as a fundamental social psychological topic.

Progress exercise

Think of two or three occasions when you have helped another person who is in need. Why did you help them? Did you help for altruistic or egoistic reasons? What about other people? Do you think all people help for the same reason as you?

Introducing anti-social behaviour

In general terms anti-social acts are those that demonstrate a lack of feeling and concern for the welfare of others. Indeed, successful social interaction and the smooth running of society can only exist if most people do not behave anti-socially. Most societies have laws therefore, enforced via a police force and a legal system, to discourage, condemn and punish anti-social acts.

So what is aggression? In its simplest form aggression is any anti-social behaviour that hurts others. Although this definition would be favoured by the Behaviourists because aggression is defined in terms of the pure behaviour of the act itself, it is inadequate because it ignores the intention behind the behaviour. It is intention that is the crucial factor in providing an adequate definition of aggression.

Suppose a child throws a ball to another child intending to start a game of catch. The other child is not watching and the ball hits the child on the head. The child cries and runs to tell the teacher about the aggressive behaviour of the other 'naughty' child. Of course the child who threw the ball is innocent but, if we have defined aggression in terms of pure behaviour, the consequences of an act, then the child who throws the ball is unfairly guilty. Clearly we need to take intention into account when we define aggression. We can now move to a more complete definition if we say that aggression is any behaviour that is *intended* to hurt others. Even this may be inadequate as there are a number of other factors that need to be taken into account, such as whether aggression always intends to hurt others.

Hostile and instrumental aggression

As a Wiganer my favourite sport is rugby league. Anyone who watches this sport could easily argue that it is a very aggressive game. But, is the aggression demonstrated by the players on the field intended to hurt the players of the other team? Well, yes, if we are honest there are incidents in many sports as well as rugby league where players do 'lose their cool' and intend to hurt others. This type of aggression we can call **hostile aggression**, which is an act of aggression with the intention of inflicting pain. In the game of rugby league the object of the game is to break through a line of defence to score a try and one way to achieve this is to take what is known as 'route one', which is to run into an opposing player and knock him or her out of the way. This action may well hurt the defending player but clearly the intention of the attacking player is not to hurt the defender. This type of aggression is known as **instrumental aggression**, which is an act of aggression with some goal other than that of inflicting pain. Some sports, such as boxing, do involve hostile aggression where the aim is to inflict pain. However, there are strict limits on where and how that pain can be inflicted. One incident on 28 June 2000 involving boxers Mike Tyson and Evander Holyfield went beyond the rules. The audience and many more watching on television saw Tyson use more than his fists during a title fight. He also used his teeth to bite Holyfield's ears! One ear was so badly damaged that Holyfield had to undergo plastic surgery to repair it. The Nevada State Boxing Commission called Tyson's behaviour 'unbecoming to a professional athlete.' It revoked Tyson's boxing licence, and demanded he pay a $3 million fine.

Anti-social aggression

One question to be addressed in this section is whether an aggressive act violates or supports the social norms of society. For example, unprovoked attacks that hurt people, such as assault, violate social norms and so this type of aggression is **anti-social**. Regrettably there are numerous examples of anti-social aggression. Consider the following tragic examples:

In 1966 Charles Whitman climbed to the top of a 307-foot tower in Austin, Texas and began firing at people walking by. Several hours later thirty-one people were wounded and fourteen dead (including Whitman, shot by the police). At that time this was the worst mass killing by a lone gunman in United States history.

Such events are not limited to the United States. On Wednesday 19 August 1987, in the village of Hungerford, England, Michael Ryan put on paramilitary kit and armed himself with a Beretta pistol, an M1 carbine and a high-velocity Kalashnikov rifle. He killed several people in his own road before shooting randomly at drivers of passing cars and anyone else unfortunate enough to be there. Finally, after killing sixteen men and women, including his own mother, he put a bullet through his own head with a handgun. Why were sixteen innocent men and women massacred on that day?

On 13 March 1996, Thomas Hamilton walked to the Dunblane Primary School in Scotland. Armed with four guns, he burst into the gymnasium where twenty-nine children were attending class. He systematically slaughtered sixteen children. Their teacher, another teacher and a dozen other pupils were wounded during the rampage. Surrounded by bodies of the dead and dying, 43-year-old Hamilton turned the gun on himself and put a bullet through his brain.

These examples are included because we are all desperate to know why these men behaved as they did. In the case of Charles Whitman his behaviour is explained by a large tumour being found in the temporal lobe of his brain. In the cases of Ryan and Hamilton, we have to examine a number of possible explanations. Perhaps more baffling are the cases where children have gone into schools, armed with weapons, and shot other children and their teachers. In February 2000 a 6-year-old boy murdered a girl in his class at school. In April 1999 Klebold and Harris shot twelve students and a teacher. In May 1998 four classmates were shot by a 15-year-old. In the latter case the boy had been expelled from school the day before.

Distinguish between anti-social and pro-social aggression.
Give an example of hostile aggression and an example of instrumental aggression (other than those in the text above).

Progress exercise

Pro-social aggression

If the police intervene in an assault and are required to use force to restrain the assailant, then although they may behave aggressively they are enforcing the social norms of society and so this type of aggression is **pro-social**. In the case of Charles Whitman it was legitimate for the police to shoot him before he could kill further innocent victims.

Sanctioned aggression

The debate surrounding sanctioned aggression has caused a great deal of controversy in the British press recently. Suppose you discover a burglar escaping through your kitchen window. You decide you must stop him or her so you reach for a kitchen knife and stab the burglar in the leg. This is **sanctioned aggression** because although you are not in a legal position to restrain the burglar (you are not the police) your behaviour would be seen to be legitimate by most people because you are upholding the social norm of maintaining law and order. In the real-life example above, the householder was merely defending his **primary territory** and so the public would view the stabbing as legitimate. However, legally, the restraining of a burglar has to be *reasonable* and if it is not the burglar has every right to challenge the legality of the attack and sue for assault. A more extreme example of sanctioned aggression involved Tony Martin early in 2000. Apparently he heard noises in his farmhouse and went downstairs to discover a 16-year-old male burglar. As the boy escaped, Tony Martin picked up his shotgun, fired and killed the burglar. In April 2000, a British jury decided his actions went beyond that considered reasonable, found him guilty of murder, and sentenced him to life imprisonment.

> **Progress review**
>
> Is pro-social aggression always for the good of society? What about the murder of more than six million Jews by the Nazis. This was considered by many Germans to be pro-social aggression as it was by order of the German Government. What are your views on this?

Psychological approaches to pro-social behaviour

A number of traditional explanations have been proposed which suggest that pro- and anti-social behaviour is either part of our genetic composition or that it is learned. This, of course, is the **nature–nurture** debate.

Specific explanations of pro-social behaviour have been provided by psychologists. Those advocating social explanations believe we all internalise a set of norms from society that we share with everyone else. Those arguing for the cognitive stance can be divided into two groups. Some psychologists emphasise the role of emotional arousal whereas others such as Latané and Darley argue that we make a number of decisions about whether or not to help. Yet another cognitive approach suggests we weigh up *the costs and benefits* and helping is the result of a logically reasoned decision-making process. Psychologists have also searched, although with little success, for *a helping personality*. Some psychologists believe that it is not the personality of the potential helper that is important but *the characteristics of the person needing help*.

In Chapter 4 evidence is presented for the view that it is the *situation* in which we find ourselves that determines our pro-social behaviours. Where we live and the influence of other *environmental factors* such as temperature, noise and odour are considered. Perhaps the most influential determinant of our behaviour is the presence of other people. Most situations have two and often many more potential helpers in attendance. Psychologists have carried out many studies, both in the laboratory and in the natural environment, to explain what have become known as *bystander effects*.

Psychological approaches to anti-social behaviour

As with pro-social behaviour a number of traditional explanations have been proposed which suggest that anti-social behaviour is either part of our genetic composition or that it is learned. A number of instinct theories have been proposed, including those by Freud and Lorenz. Alternatively some psychologists, such as Bandura, believe that all behaviour is learned and, of course, this includes anti-social behaviour. In the 1930s Dollard et al. proposed that aggression was always the result of frustration and this provoked a significant amount of research. Berkowitz in particular proposed the '**weapons effect**', suggesting that the mere presence of weapons implied aggression. This may well be the case for mass murderers such as Ryan and Hamilton mentioned above. In contrast to these 'social' explanations, others emphasise cognitive processing. Zillmann proposed that a combination of arousal and cognitive factors explain aggressive behaviour more clearly. Social constructionist approaches consider that aggression can only be understood within the context in which it occurs and that the way in which a person interprets a situation is very important.

Yet further theories consider that anti-social behaviour is the result of a particular type of personality. Such 'individual approaches' also consider the role of alcohol and possible gender differences. In contrast there are '**deindividuational** approaches' where it is suggested that the individual loses responsibility when part of a group. Finally, the role that environmental factors may play on anti-social behaviour is considered.

Further reading

Keneally, T. (1994) *Schindler's List*. London: Hodder and Stoughton. Fictionalised history: the full story of Oskar Schindler. An excellent read. The film, also called *Schindler's List* (directed by Steven Spielberg, 1993), is equally excellent.

Frank, A. *The Diary of a Young Girl: The Definitive Edition*. Harmondsworth: Penguin. *The Diary of Anne Frank*. Original publication 1947. Amazing tale and compulsive reading. Emphasis in this chapter is the behaviour of those who helped the Frank family.

Rosenthal, A.M. (1999) *Thirty-eight Witnesses: The Kitty Genovese Case*. Berkeley: University of California Press. Updated review of the tragic tale. Original publication (1964) New York: McGraw Hill. The Kitty Genovese tragedy has also been made into a film, entitled *Death Scream*.

The film, *Flight 90: Disaster on the Potomac* (1984) is a feature film portraying the event and the rescue of Priscilla Tirado by Lenny Skutnik and Arland Williams, Director Michael Lewis.

Section I

PRO-SOCIAL
BEHAVIOUR

2

Traditional explanations of pro-social behaviour

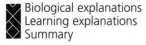

Biological explanations
Learning explanations
Summary

Biological explanations

Natural selection

Is a willingness to help others an inherited characteristic? According to the theory of evolution proposed by Charles Darwin, behaviours are naturally selected if they promote survival and reproduction. A behaviour that is costly therefore should not be selected. Individuals with such traits would not reproduce and so we should not observe altruism in the animal world. However, acts of altruistic behaviour have been observed in many species of animal: rabbits, bees, wasps, termites, birds and dolphins as well as humans. This is known as the 'paradox of altruism' and according to natural selection it should not exist, but it does.

Reciprocal altruism

The 'paradox of altruism' is explained by Trivers (1971) by what he calls **reciprocal altruism**. Trivers believes that a seemingly altruistic act for another can benefit the helping individual. He argues that if a member of a species helps another, then as long as the receiving animal remembers the event it may well repay the favour in the future and so this will benefit both those involved and hence altruistic behaviour has survival benefits.

Kin selection

Instead of considering natural selection in terms of the survival of the individual animal, it is believed that it is the survival of the **genotype**, the survival of a genetic relative, that is more important. Thus an animal may sacrifice itself to save the genes of its relatives. This is known as *kin selection*. In evolutionary terms this means that the strongest genes survive: not the survival of the fittest individual, but the fittest genes. This is often called **inclusive fitness**. So each individual is motivated not only to live long enough to pass on his or her individual genes but also to enhance the reproductive odds for those who share some of those same genes. Sociobiologists such as Wilson (1975) argue that this does not apply exclusively to animals but that it is built into the genetic code of humans too.

Genetic determinism

Rushton (1989) goes even further and proposes a **genetic determinism** model. He believes that we do not mate with random strangers but that we seek out lovers and spouses who are genetically similar to ourselves. It then follows that we are more likely to help those whom we perceive as genetically similar to ourselves, because we have inherited our ancestors' assumption that this would be the most effective guarantee that similar genes would survive. Of course, those with most genetic similarity are our immediate family, followed by close relatives, and it is these whom we make it our priority to help before others. Support for this view is provided in a study by Burnstein, Crandall and Kitayama performed in 1994. Not surprisingly they found that when in a situation such as a house fire, people reported that they were much more likely to help relatives than non-relatives.

Evaluation

The study by Burnstein et al. can be evaluated as having a strength in that their results can be generalised because they studied males as well as females and their studies were carried out in both Japan and America. However, the question is raised as to whether people help their relatives because of the genetic link or simply because they love them. Evolutionary psychologists would simply explain this as being the same thing: we love our immediate family because of the genetic link, and they would argue further that helping genetically similar relatives before others can also be shown in animals such as bees (although it is not known whether bees love each other). Greenberg (1979) demonstrated that bees guarding a hive will admit close relatives before those who are more distantly related.

Despite this, evolutionary psychologists still struggle to answer the question of why we help complete strangers with whom we do not share some of the same genes. Rushton also has the problem of explaining how we perceive that people we help are genetically similar to ourselves. Rushton suggests that those whose appearance and behaviour is like our own may well be genetically similar to us. However, others such as Anderson (1989) argue that the only way we can determine genetic similarity is to give a blood test and clearly this is not possible when faced with an emergency situation.

Explain what is meant by the terms reciprocal altruism, kin selection, genetic determinism.

Progress exercise

Learning explanations

Learning Theory

According to Rheingold (1982) children as young as 18 months frequently help others. How have they acquired this behaviour? From a learning (nurture) point of view, it is argued that pro-social behaviour is learned in the same way as any other behaviour. This can be achieved in three ways:

1 for parents and others to reward pro-social acts with praise;
2 for parents to act as pro-social models themselves;
3 to expose children to other models who behave in pro-social ways.

Support for these suggestions is provided in studies which have shown that pro-social acts are more likely to occur when they are rewarded and Moss and Page (1972) have shown that helping behaviour decreases when it is punished. Midlarsky et al. (1973) found that the best way to teach children pro-social behaviour is to have a child observe it and then reward the child when it is copied. Mere reward is insufficient; what does strengthen the likelihood of a repetition of the behaviour is the *type* of reward given. It has been found that 'dispositional praise' where the child is encouraged specifically is much more effective than 'global praise' where the reinforcer is nothing more than a simple 'well done'. A study by Mills and Grusec (1989) demonstrated precisely this with children aged 8 and 9 years. It involved children playing a game with tokens that could be exchanged for toys. As tokens were won all children were encouraged to give some of their tokens to poor children. As they did, the children were given one of two types of praise: either the general 'that was a nice and helpful thing to do' or the dispositional 'you're a nice and helpful person'. As you may expect, when the children were later playing the game again and could share with others or not, those who had been given dispositional praise were significantly more likely to share than those given the global praise.

Imitating models has been shown to work not only for children but also for adults. Bryan and Test (1967) created a situation where motorists passed a stationary car where in one condition a man was helping a woman motorist change a wheel and in another condition the woman was receiving no help from anyone. Several hundred metres along the road there was another woman requiring help with a puncture. Of the 4,000 passing cars, Bryan and Test found 50 per cent more motorists stopped to help the woman after passing the model than in a second condition where there was no model.

Progress exercise

List three ways in which pro-social behaviour can be learned.
What is the difference between dispositional praise and global praise?

Evaluation

Three questions need to be asked:

1 Do children merely exhibit demand characteristics or are they really behaving altruistically?
2 Is the learning of pro-social behaviour transferable from one situation to another?
3 What exactly is meant by learning?

There could well be a fundamental problem here, which is that if children are rewarded too frequently they will believe it is valuable to help someone in need only when they get a reward for doing so. Put another way, rather than encouraging altruism over-emphasising rewards can easily lead to helping that is due to egoism. A study by Rushton (1975) was designed to investigate this dilemma. In this study children played a bowling game in which they won tokens. Some children observed an adult model keep all the tokens he won and in another condition different children observed the model put half the tokens won into a jar for Bobby (a needy child) as part of a Save the Children campaign. As you might expect, the children observing the generous adult were more generous than the children in the other group. The question to be asked is 'Were the generous children behaving altruistically or were they merely feeling the pressure of the experimental situation forcing them to donate tokens to Bobby?' To answer this question Rushton conducted a second study using the same children but modifying the design in three ways: the model did not bowl or donate; the charity was different; and the study was conducted some two months after the original. Given these changes Rushton believed that any donating would be altruistically motivated. Rushton found precisely what he expected: the children who had observed the original model donate to the charity gave more than the children who had not. The children thus behaved altruistically, a behaviour that they had learned.

If children learn to behave pro-socially then one could comfortably assume that once learned, it could be applied whenever needed (as in the Rushton study). To make this assumption is wrong. Many studies have shown that children who behave pro-socially in one situation do not do so in another. Although dated, the work of Hartshorne and May (1929) found the correlation between helping in one situation and helping in another was only 0.23. Many years later, and in a different culture, Magoo and Khanna (1991) found that students, at Indian Universities, who were rated as highly altruistic were no more likely to donate blood than students rated as low on measures of altruism. It appears that although learning plays an important part there are many other factors to take into account.

Green and Schneider (1974) agree that helping behaviour is learned but they question exactly what that learning is. They argue that children learn the capacity to recognise and appreciate the needs of others and acquire an understanding of 'societal prescriptions'. What determines their altruism then is not necessarily the mere observation and imitation of others but their ability to take the point of view of other people.

Age differences and helping

Whilst it is argued that children as young as 18 months frequently help others, this has not been tested under experimental conditions. Using a procedure similar to that of Latané and Darley in their 'lady in distress' study (1970) it has been discovered that children go through stages in which helping increases and then decreases. Staub (1979) had children of various ages wait in a room for a few minutes. Whilst they were waiting the children heard a crash from the next room followed by the sound of a crying child. Staub found that the child leaving the room in which they had been asked to wait, taken as a measure of seeking to help the child in distress, varied with age. Staub found that willingness to help first increased with age and then decreased. He suggested that the reason for this was the inability of young children to empathise with others, but as they get older they are more capable of putting themselves in another's place and so are more likely to help in an emergency. However, as they get older, children become more sensitive to criticism which makes them less likely to help as they fear adult criticism. As will be shown in Chapter 5, adults show **audience inhibition** where they are less likely to help in the presence of others.

More evidence that altruistic behaviour increases with age is provided in a study by Green and Schneider (1974). They placed boys into four age-group categories: 5–6, 7–8, 9–10 and 13–14. They then provided the boys with opportunities first to share sweets with classmates and second to help an experimenter who had dropped a number of pencils. They found (as can be seen in Table 2.1) that both sharing and helping increased with age.

Table 2.1 **Helping behaviour increases with age**

	age group (in years)			
Altruistic response	5-6	7-8	9-10	13-14
% of sweets shared	60	92	100	100
% who picked up pencils	48	76	100	96

Summary

In this chapter the two traditional approaches of nature and nurture have been considered in relation to pro-social behaviour. The nature view argues that pro-social behaviour is inherited and is part of our genetic make-up. Rushton (1989), for example, argues that our specific genes determine that we will automatically help those who are genetically similar to ourselves. Whether this is true is debatable as Rushton has little empirical support for his view.

Those proposing the nurture argument believe that all behaviour is learned, of which pro-social behaviour is one aspect. Many studies have shown that children who observe a model behave pro-socially imitate the behaviour. It is also suggested that pro-social behaviour increases with age and it is linked to the ability to empathise with others. A number of questions are raised in relation to the learning approach, such as what exactly learning is and whether children can transfer what they have learned in one situation to another.

Although these traditional explanations make a relevant contribution, they compete with a number of theories proposed specifically to explain altruism and helping behaviour.

Review exercise

Describe two pieces of evidence that suggest pro-social behaviour may be learned.

Compare and contrast with evidence suggesting that pro-social behaviour may not be learned.

Further reading

Grusec, J.E. (1992) Social learning theory and developmental psychology: the legacy of Robert Sears and Albert Bandura. *Developmental Psychology* 28, 776–786. An in-depth look at Bandura and learning theory.

Manning, A. and Dawkins, M.S. (1998) *An Introduction to Animal Behaviour* (5th edn) Cambridge: Cambridge University Press. Readable and up-to-date text for more on biological explanations.

3

Social-psychological explanations of pro-social behaviour

 Norm theories
Empathy and arousal in pro-social behaviour
Cognitive explanations of pro-social behaviour
Summary

Norm theories

In this chapter theories proposed specifically to explain pro-social behaviour are examined. The first, known as norm theories, do not look at pro-social behaviour from the viewpoint of each individual but take a much wider perspective and consider that pro-social behaviour is something that is learned by every member of a society as part of a set of socialised norms. These **socialised norms** are unwritten rules that tell us how to behave in various situations. They are social guidelines, a set of norms or societal standards for behaviour that represent the consensus about which behaviours are acceptable and encouraged and those which are unacceptable and discouraged. Norm theorists consider that all norms are internalised through the socialisation process.

Norm theorists argue that pro-social behaviour is that which benefits society as a whole and we help others because we are motivated to act in accordance with the norm for helping those in need.

Reciprocity norm

The specific norm for helping those in need is said by Gouldner (1960) to be the norm of reciprocity. This **reciprocity norm** is where we feel morally obliged to help those who have helped us. It is common in many cultures for people to think 'scratch my back and I'll scratch yours' and in everyday life we often 'owe a favour' to someone who has helped us. A demonstration of the reciprocity norm operating on an individual level was shown in a study by Regan in 1968. Pairs of participants (actually one accomplice and one participant) took part in a study rating a series of pictures. During the break three experimental conditions came into play:

1 the accomplice returned and gave a Coke to the participant with the comment, 'The experimenter said it was okay, so I brought one for you too.'
2 the experimenter gave both the accomplice and participant a Coke saying, 'I brought you guys a Coke.'
3 no drinks were provided.

The theory is that participants in the first condition had a favour done for them and according to Gouldner they would feel morally obliged to reciprocate, more so than in conditions 2 or 3. As the rating of the pictures continued, the accomplice wrote a note to the participant explaining that he was selling raffle tickets and would the participant like to buy one. The dependent variable is the mean number of raffle tickets bought by the participant. Table 3.1 shows the results: the

Table 3.1 The reciprocity norm in action

	experimental condition		
	accomplice gave drink	experimenter gave drink	no drink
mean no. of raffle tickets bought	1.75	1.05	0.95

Source: adapted from Regan 1968

participant reciprocated the favour and bought more raffle tickets than when the favour did not need to be reciprocated.

It is a little more complicated than this, however. Reciprocity can occur on different levels. If we can we do favours for our friends who will probably return the favour, but also, although less powerful, we can do favours at a wider level when we help people whom we are unlikely ever to meet again and who will never be able to reciprocate. This is precisely what the reciprocity norm is all about – if everyone has internalised the reciprocity norm then our favours for others will be returned by others and all people will help all other people. This view is supported by the results of the Regan study above. Whilst participants did buy more raffle tickets for the person buying them a Coke, it is also true that participants in all groups bought a raffle ticket even though the accomplice had not done a favour for them previously.

Evaluation

In evaluation of Gouldner's theory it may well be the case that we do a favour for a friend or neighbour and that we also give assistance to people we will never see again and will never be able to reciprocate. But not everyone behaves like this. Some of our 'friends' do not return favours and clearly not everyone helps others. This means that either the reciprocity norm is not internalised by all, or there are other factors in action.

Another problem is that of **self-serving bias** where we generally perceive others' level of co-operation to be lower than it really is and our own level of co-operation to be higher than it really is. Put another way, we tend to under-match the level of co-operation others demonstrate. In this way Gouldner's theory does not match everyday behaviour. We should also remember that there is more to a reciprocity norm than pro-social behaviour; we often seek revenge if someone aggresses against us and we may even encourage our children to reciprocate when hit by another child.

Social responsibility norm

An alternative norm theory is that proposed in 1963 by Berkowitz and Daniels. They suggest we have a **social responsibility norm** whereby we help those in need because they are dependent on us. As a result we help the ubiquitous old lady to cross the road because she is dependent on us and we feel a social responsibility to help her. Norms such as this, as well as many others, are claimed to be universal and essential for successful interaction amongst people in any society. If it is the case that we have a social responsibility norm, then in an emergency situation all witnesses should offer help as somebody is in need and the social responsibility norm is elicited in the observers. Plainly this is not the case.

Evaluation

If the social responsibility norm is elicited, then why do some people not help? There are three possible explanations:

1 It may be because the norm has not been learned by all, even though Berkowitz and Daniels claim it and other norms are universal.
2 Another possibility is that the social responsibility norm is one of many that an individual possesses and in any situation an individual is faced with conflicting norms: the norm of *mind your own business* conflicting with *social responsibility*, for example.
3 It may be because the norms are too general and do not apply to specific situations. That is, we may possess the norms but we do not know how to apply them in a given situation.

Personalised Norms

In response to the criticisms of socialised norms, Schwartz (1977) suggests instead that we should consider **personalised norms**. Such norms relate to an individual's feelings of moral obligation and Schwartz's concern is to explain how such norms become activated for an individual in a given situation. His *theory of norm activation* (Figure 3.1) attempts to predict when people will act on their personalised norms.

In the *activation* stage a person becomes aware of another's need and perceives that there are actions he or she could undertake to help. The person then feels a moral *obligation* to help, either through an existing personal norm or by constructing a new one. The person then begins to assess the costs involved and may attempt to deny

ACTIVATION
Perception of need and personal responsibility

awareness that a person is needing help
perception that action could be of use
recognition that one's own ability could play a part
apprehension of participating

OBLIGATION
norm construction and feelings of moral obligation

awareness of existence of personal norms
feelings of moral obligation generated

DEFENCES
assessment, evaluation and reassessment of response

assessment of costs and possible outcomes
if outcomes outweigh feelings of obligation, no help given
reassessment and redefinition:
state of need; responsibility to respond; suitability of norm activated.

RESPONSE

action taken if defences are minimal
No action taken if defences outweigh moral obligation

Figure 3.1 **The Schwartz theory of norm activation**

responsibility. This is the *defence* stage. Finally, the person makes a *response* which is to help or not to help.

Evaluation

One advantage of the Schwartz model is that it specifies how motivation to help is activated in a situation and how defences come into play to determine whether or not help will be given. Defences will be activated when helping may do more harm than good. We may well think initially that we can help a motorcyclist after an accident by removing her helmet to check her breathing, for example. But then we assess the suitability of the norm activated and reassess the situation. As our action of removing the helmet may well do more harm than good a *negative personal norm* comes into play and we do not remove the helmet.

This theory suffers in the same way as other norm theories do in that:

1 The number of norms available to us is vast; there are so many and they are so vague that they can be used to explain almost anything.
2 Norms may be in conflict: for example the 'social responsibility' norm may conflict with the norm for 'minding your own business'.
3 It may well be that we need a new norm for each situation we encounter.

Progress exercise

Briefly summarise what is meant by: the reciprocity norm, the social responsibility norm, norm activation. List three weaknesses of norm theories.

Empathy and arousal in pro-social behaviour

Introduction

Consider the situation of the Flight 90 disaster. Lenny Skutnik witnessed the horrific accident that presumably aroused powerful emotions in him. As he watched and saw Priscilla Tirado struggling, he may have imagined how he would feel if he himself were in that position. This is **empathy**, defined as the vicarious experiencing of another person's emotions. That is, we take the perspective of the person in need and this produces emotional arousal. In Skutnik's case it was clear what action he had to take: he jumped into the river to save her. The crucial question is 'Why did he behave in the way he did?' To provide an answer to this question we need to return to the debate outlined earlier which presented the alternatives of egoism and altruism. Did Lenny help for egoistic (selfish) reasons or did he help for the ultimate goal of benefiting Priscilla Tirado? Let us consider the egoistic options that are available to us in an emergency situation:

1 If we help we will avoid other observers thinking negatively of us ('If I don't help others will think badly of me'), or we will avoid thinking negatively about ourselves ('If I don't help I'm not a very nice person'). This is known *as empathy-specific punishment.*
2 If we help we may well obtain some praise or reward from others ('Others will tell me how kind and brave I am'). This is known as *empathy-specific reward.*
3 If we avoid the situation by simply walking away we can reduce our emotional arousal but if we help we can also reduce our emotional arousal. Both of these involve *aversive arousal reduction.*

The third egoistic explanation, that of aversive arousal reduction, is the elimination of the negative feelings elicited by the situation. It is unlikely though that any negative feelings we experience will be reduced by walking away, because the plight of the victim still remains. It is much more likely that we will help him or her because this will eliminate *our* negative emotion and help him or her too. As Hoffman (1981) puts it, 'empathic distress is unpleasant and helping the victim is usually the best way to get rid of the source'. So we help the victim not because we feel for them but to help ourselves obtain relief from our negative state.

On observing the plight of Priscilla Tirado, Lenny Skutnik, in a state of high emotional arousal, had a number of options. He could avoid the situation and walk away but may well have had the vision and memory of a dying person with him for the rest of his life. If he jumped into the river to save Priscilla Tirado he would at the same time avoid empathy-specific punishment, possibly gain empathy-specific reward and, of course, release himself from his highly emotional state. This explanation has been developed into the negative state relief model.

The Negative state relief model

The argument here is that we help not through concern for the welfare of others but through a concern to make ourselves feel better; to reduce our own negative feelings. Cialdini et al. (1981) outline what they call the **negative state relief model**, outlined in Figure 3.2.

Experimental support

To test their model Cialdini et al. (1987) had students listen to a tape-recording of another student who had asked for help with her work. Half the participants heard a 'high-empathy' version (which included a plea to imagine how they would feel if they were not helped in the same situation). The other half of the participants heard a 'low-empathy' version (they were told to listen to the tape but not concern themselves with the student's feelings). Another variable was then introduced which was to provide the participants with information suggesting that helping would or would not improve their mood. The study was interested in the number of participants from each condition offering to help the student with her work. The negative state relief model would predict that those in the high-empathy group would be more likely to help than those in the low-empathy condition, and the results of the study confirmed this. More importantly, the negative state relief model predicts that people help only to improve their own mood. This is exactly what was found: the participants who believed their mood would be improved were much more likely to offer help than the students who did not believe their mood would be improved.

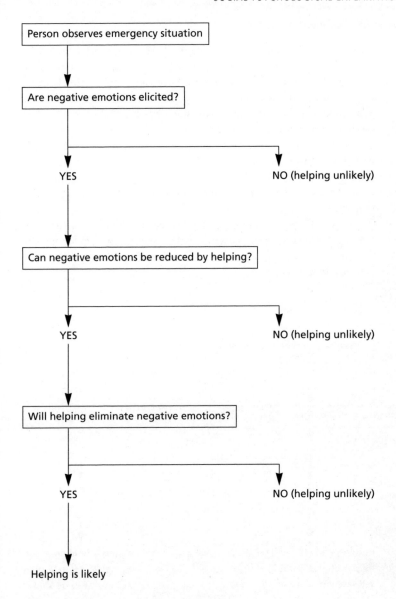

Figure 3.2 **The negative state relief model**

Source: adapted from R.A. Baron and D. Byrne 1994

The empathy–altruism model

On theoretical grounds, both Coke et al. (1978) and Batson (1981, 1991) refute the view that we help in order to reduce our own negative feelings. Their belief is that we help not because of egoism but because of pure altruism where our only goal is to help the person in need. This model is in agreement with the negative state relief that in an emergency situation we experience empathy and this produces emotional arousal. However, the models then differ because the empathy–altruism model believes that the empathy we experience then motivates us *to reduce the distress of the person in need by helping them*. Batson et al. (1991) call this the **empathy–altruism hypothesis** (Figure 3.3).

Despite Batson's believing that altruism is the prime reason for helping, it can be seen from the model that people may help for egoistic reasons. As he puts it, 'the fragile flower of selfless altruism can easily be crushed by self concern'.

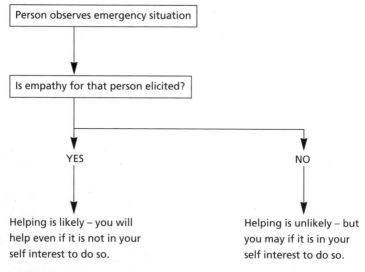

Figure 3.3 **The empathy–altruism hypothesis**

Source: adapted from Aronson et al. 1999

Experimental support

Is there any experimental support for the empathy–altruism model? A study conducted by Dovidio et al. in 1990 used the same procedure as in the Cialdini et al. study, in that a student described a problem she faced with her work. Again there is a high-empathy condition (participants told to imagine how she felt about her problem) and a low-empathy condition (participants told to focus on what she said and not her feelings). The reason for this difference is that the empathy–altruism model predicts that people help to relieve the other person's problem. It follows, of course, that if the other person's problem cannot be resolved then people will not help. The participants were later given the opportunity to help the girl with either the same problem that caused the original empathy or with another problem. The results of the study by Dovidio et al. provide strong support for the empathy–altruism model. It was found (see Table 3.2) that those in the high-empathy condition did help more than those in the low-empathy condition but, crucially, only when they could assist with the problem which caused the empathy originally.

The empathic-joy hypothesis

Two models have now been presented, each taking the opposite end of the altruism–egoism continuum. An alternative model proposed by Smith et al. (1989) represents a compromise between these two models. They suggest, in their **empathic-joy hypothesis**, that it is indeed emotional arousal that leads us to help. However, rather than

Table 3.2 **Percentage of participants offering to help a student with a problem**

	same problem	different problem
high empathy	62.2%	33.7%
low empathy	33.7%	45.9%

Source: adapted from Dovidio et. al. 1990

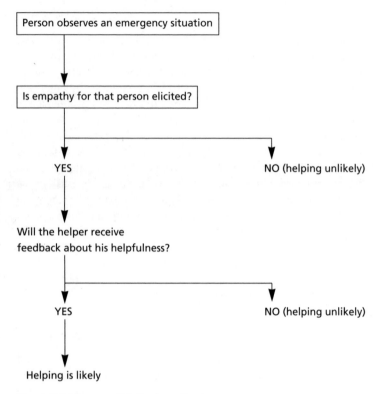

Figure 3.4 **The empathic-joy hypothesis**

Source: adapted from R.A. Baron and D. Byrne 1994

helping to reduce our negative emotion, we behave pro-socially to experience the joy our positive action will bring.

Empathic joy in children

Many psychologists believe that empathy is learned and, without it, altruism would probably be impossible (see Chapter 2). Although a child may develop empathic responses without becoming altruistic, a child is unlikely to be altruistic unless he or she develops empathy first. Is it possible therefore, to teach empathy? Midlarsky and Bryan (1967) conditioned primary-school-age girls by having a woman experimenter hug them and express joy when prizes were donated. The assumption was that this would make the girls feel happy and lead them to empathise with the obvious pleasure expressed by the experimenter. As a control, some girls were not hugged by the experimenter, and in a third condition some girls were hugged by an experimenter who did not express joy. The girls who had been hugged by a joyful experimenter were later found to make larger anonymous donations to poor children than did other girls. There was no difference between the girls in the other two groups. What seems to be necessary, therefore, is not the mere presence of a hug, but when the hug is an expression of the joy experienced.

Think about your own behaviour. Give three examples of situations where you have helped or have not helped someone in need. State which of the above models would explain your behaviour in each case and why you think the model would explain it.

Progress exercise

Cognitive explanations of pro-social behaviour

Whereas norm theories consider internalised and universal beliefs and empathic arousal emphasises physiological emotions, cognitive models consider helping or not helping to be the result of a logical decision-making process: how the observer perceives a situation, assesses available factors and, on the basis of balancing the pertinent factors, makes a decision whether to help or not.

The Latané and Darley cognitive model

Latané and Darley's five-stage model (1970) looks at the decisions involved in perceiving a situation and the consequences of particular actions (Figure 3.5).

Many studies support the existence of each of these decisions, including many conducted in the laboratory by Latané and Darley themselves in addition to others. Shotland and Huston (1979) have

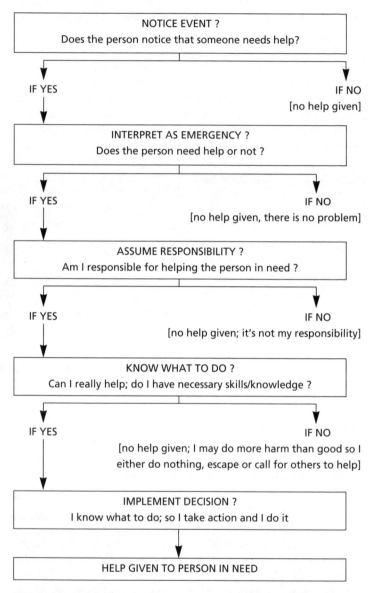

Figure 3.5 **The Latané and Darley cognitive model of helping**

Source: Adapted from B. Latané and J.M. Darley 1970

identified five characteristics that lead us to perceive that an event is an emergency:

1 something happens which is sudden and unexpected;
2 there is clear threat of harm to the person;
3 the harm will persist or worsen if no one intervenes;
4 the victim is helpless and needs outside assistance;
5 some form of effective assistance is possible.

Experimental support

Other studies (e.g. Bickman 1972) have shown that the more ambiguous the situation is, the less likely it is that help will be offered. Clark and Word (1974) found that an observer's uncertainty with respect to the seriousness of the consequences to the victim may be crucial. In their study they found that participants in emergency situations were less likely to intervene and, if they did so, were much slower than were participants in unambiguous emergency situations. Their study involved an actor playing the role of an incompetent electrician who, after receiving an electric shock from a faulty control box, falls off his ladder. Participants were divided into three groups:

1 unambiguous condition: 'electrician' in full view of most participants called for help before passing out. This was a clear and unambiguous emergency situation.
2 moderately ambiguous condition: here the 'electrician' fell behind a counter but still called for help before passing out. This was moderately ambiguous because, although most participants saw him fall and heard his cry for help, they did not see him become unconscious.
3 ambiguous condition: here he fell behind the counter but made no further sound. Participants therefore did not hear him call for help and they did not see him become unconscious.

The question for all participants is: does the 'electrician' need help or not?

Before considering the results it is worth mentioning that Clark and Word introduced another variable, which is whether the 'electrician' was touching a live wire (high danger) or not (low danger). This presents an additional set of factors which is whether the benefit of giving help will outweigh the cost of not helping: the higher the risk to participants the less likely they are to help. See the section on cost–benefit analysis below.

As can be seen in Table 3.3, the results of the study show that the rate of helping is high if a situation is unambiguous but the more ambiguous the situation the less likely it is that people will help.

In a study by Shotland and Straw (1976) it was found that people are more likely to help if they believe an assault victim does not know the attacker. In their study, participants were completing questionnaires when they heard, outside in the corridor, a loud fight between two people (which was staged by students from the drama department). In one condition, the 'married condition', the woman screamed 'I don't even know why I ever married you!' which led to only 19 per cent of participants intervening. In the other 'stranger' condition, where participants heard 'I don't know you', led to 65 per cent of participants intervening directly.

Evaluation

Although Latané and Darley's model describes the decisions a person is likely to go through, it is questionable as to what extent it applies

Table 3.3 Percentage of participants helping an 'electrician' in various situations

	Percentage of participants who gave assistance	
	low danger%	high danger%
Unambiguous	100	over 90
moderately ambiguous	over 50	less than 50
ambiguous	50 if in pairs	very few if alone

to real life. In an emergency situation will people have time to make so many decisions? It has also been argued that it is surprising that anyone ever helps given all the chances provided by this model for a person to opt out of helping.

Attributions and helping

Yet another important factor to consider is what we perceive to be the cause of an incident. If a person needing help is perceived to be in the predicament because it is his own fault (they may elicit an emotion of disgust or condemnation in us) then we are less likely to help than if we perceive that the victim is not responsible for his plight (where the emotion of empathy may be elicited) and helping is more likely. For example, if you witness a car accident where one car has pulled out of a side road into the path of another, you are more likely to go to the assistance of the innocent driver before you go to help the driver responsible for the accident. This is what Lerner (1975) called the '**just world**' **hypothesis**. As he puts it 'We want to believe we live in a world where people get what they deserve or, rather, deserve what they get' (207).

Cost–benefit Analysis

An alternative cognitive theory is the cost–benefit analysis, originally outlined by Homans (1961) as the social exchange theory but developed and applied by Piliavin et al. (1981) to explain the results of their 'subway samaritan study' (detailed later in this section). This theory suggests that we try to maximise the ratio of our social rewards to the ratio of our social costs and so whether we help or not depends on the outcome of a weighing-up of both the costs and benefits of helping.

The *costs of helping* may include:

- effort: helping may be physically demanding;
- time: we may be late for work or an appointment;
- loss of resources: we may damage clothes, or lose earnings;
- risk of harm: we may be put in physical danger or suffer pain;
- negative emotional response: we may feel physically sick.

All these factors are weighed against the *benefits of helping:*

- social approval: thanks from victim (and crowd if there is one);
- self-esteem: feeling that one is a kind person;
- positive emotional response: feelings (such as elation) elicited by successful rescue.

Further, it is argued by Piliavin et al., such a cost–benefit analysis is performed to reduce negative emotional arousal and, in addition to the above factors, the *costs of not helping* must be assessed. These can include:

- disapproval: no rewards from victim or crowd;
- damaged self-esteem: feelings that one is not a kind person;
- negative emotional response: not helping may cause feelings of guilt.

Support for cost–benefit analysis

The Piliavin et al. model has a number of supporting studies which suggest that increasing various costs can lead to a decrease in helping, whilst increasing the benefits can lead to an increase in helping. In work organisations the beneficiaries of helpers can include their co-workers, customers, or the organisation as a whole. Help may be in the form of helping someone catch up on paperwork, or lifting a heavy object. A study performed by Wright et al. (1993) looked at helping in relation to the cost–reward matrix. In their study, students were paid to find and correct errors embedded in order forms. They were paid either an hourly rate (regardless of how well they did) or paid a bonus but only if they completed the task. Wright et al. also varied the task difficulty, making it either relatively easy, moderately difficult or difficult. As they worked, the students were joined by a late arrival (a confederate) who repeatedly asked for assistance. Did the student participants help the late arrival? Results showed that least help was given when the task was difficult and where they were paid only if they completed the task. In other words, the students did not give help to the late arrival when it was costly to themselves. Which group of students helped the late arrival most? It was those in the difficult condition who were paid hourly. These students would be paid whether they completed the task or not; helping cost them nothing. You might note that this is yet another approach which suggests that helping (or not helping) is a selfish act. According to this theory, we only help when the benefits outweigh the costs, and if they do not we simply do not help!

It is interesting to observe how people behave when they are confronted with a person shaking a charity collecting box. Yes, this is a good way of donating to charity but people often prefer not to be challenged in this way and often people who have already given to several charities on the same day and sometimes even in the same street do not want to give again. What do people do to avoid a direct confrontation between themselves and the collector? As discovered in a study by Pancer et al. (1979), people simply walked further around the collector, and as the collecting demand increased so did the extra distance walked. Specifically, the study by Pancer et al. included several variables each with an increased demand. Of least demand was nothing more than a table with a collecting box; of moderate demand was when a person was at the table with a collecting box and the high-demand condition was when the person with the collecting box was handicapped.

As can be seen, people avoid helping by increasing the distance between them and the collector; in this way there is no monetary cost, but there is the cost of walking a few extra metres in avoidance.

Piliavin et al. also suggest that the cost–benefit analysis for each individual may be very different for, as will be seen later, factors associated with the potential helper must be taken into account as well as factors associated with the victim.

Summary

In this chapter theories proposed specifically to explain pro-social behaviour have been presented. Norm theorists believe that everyone internalises the values of society and behaves pro-socially either because of a reciprocity norm or because of a social responsibility norm. Schwartz outlines how such norms become activated in an individual. Norm theories struggle to explain why not every person responds equally when a norm has been activated, but explain this by suggesting that other norms, such as the one for 'minding one's own business', come into play.

An alternative approach postulates that any action (or inaction) is the extent of *emotional arousal* an emergency situation creates in us. We can help to reduce our level of arousal or we can avoid potentially emotive situations, which might also reduce our level of arousal. This is the *negative state relief model*. In both these cases we act for egoistic reasons. The empathy–altruism model proposes that it is the empathy we feel for a person that determines our behaviour. The empathic-joy hypothesis takes this further, believing we help for selfish reasons through the joy we experience by helping. Cognitive models, such as those proposed by Latané and Darley and Piliavin et al., believe we go through a logical series of decisions, possibly weighing up the costs and rewards of helping and/or not helping.

Review exercise

1. Construct a table which summarises three differences between the negative-state relief model, the empathy-altruism model and the empathic-joy hypothesis.
2. Describe one norm theory and one piece of supporting evidence. Describe one cognitive model and one piece of supporting evidence.

Further reading

Batson, C.D. (1991) *The Altruism Question: Towards a Social Psychological Answer*. Hillsdale, NJ: Erlbaum. Good review of latest thinking on empathy and altruism.

Aronson, E. et al. (1999) *Social Psychology* 3rd edn, (Harlow: Longman.) Chapter 11 has a good review of norm theories, empathy and altruism.

Individual and environmental explanations of pro-social behaviour

Personal determinants of helping
Gender and cultural differences in pro-social behaviour
Situational determinants of helping behaviour
Pro-social behaviour and environmental psychology

Personal determinants of helping: who helps whom?

Helping behaviour may be due neither to a complex decision-making process nor to emotions nor to internalised norms. It may be attributable to our personality. It may simply be due to the situation in which we find ourselves, and be determined by environmental factors. Such factors may also vary according to the culture we are in.

Characteristics of the potential helper

Is there a helping personality? In a study by Huston et al. (1981), where 32 helpers who had intervened were interviewed, it was found that, compared to non-helpers, they were taller, heavier and were more able to cope with emergencies in that they had been trained in some medical/first aid capacity. Clark and Word (1974) found 90 per cent of those with 'electrical' experience helped a person who had apparently suffered an electric shock, and Cramer et al. (1988) found

Table 4.1 The components of the helping personality	
Characteristics of those who help	*Characteristics of those who do not help*
• had high internal locus of control	• had low internal locus of control
• held belief in a 'just world'	• held less belief in a 'just world'
• felt socially responsible	• felt less socially responsible
• possessed ability to empathise	• possessed less ability to empathise
• were less egocentric	• were more egocentric

Source: Adapted from Bierhoff, Klein and Kramp 1991

nurses were more likely to offer assistance than were students. In an attempt to identify the components of a helping personality, Bierhoff et al. (1991) compared those who witnessed a road traffic accident and provided first aid with those who witnessed such an accident and did not provide first aid. The results of this study are shown in Table 4.1.

Is helping related to religious beliefs? Are religious people more likely to help someone in need than someone who is not religious? Apparently not, according to work by Batson et al. (1981) who found that the mere fact of going to church is not a good predictor of future helping behaviour. Helping may not be related to religious beliefs but it has been shown to be related to morality. Studies of people who have saved the lives of others often find they have deeply held moral values. Viktor Orekhov, a former Soviet KGB officer, saved hundreds of people from arrest and interrogation by secretly informing them of planned KGB action. When asked why he had risked his life for the Russian dissidents his reply was that, unless he acted, his children would be ashamed of him.

Maruyama et al. (1982) found that if a person is made personally responsible then they are more likely to help. In this study children were 'trick-or-treating' on Hallowe'en. When the children arrived at a particular house they were asked to donate sweets to a children's hospital. There were three conditions:

1   maximum responsibility: the donated sweets had the child's name written on the bag;
2   moderate responsibility: where one child was made responsible for the entire group;
3   no responsibility: where no child had his or her name on the bag.

The results (see Figure 4.1) show that the greater the personal responsibility the more sweets were donated.

Studies have shown that those with appropriate skills are more likely to help: where there are no other people present, individuals will still help despite their lack of competence. Where other people are present, a whole new set of factors apply in determining whether or not help will be given. These are known as 'bystander effects' which are considered in greater depth later.

Helping and mood

The mood of the bystander should logically be a significant factor in whether help is given or not. We might assume that being in a good mood increases the chances of helping. Isen and Levin (1972) put participants in a good mood by having them find money in a telephone

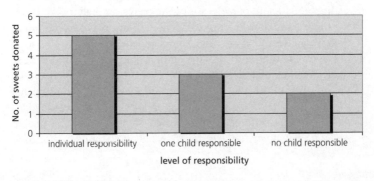

Figure 4.1 **Decreasing personal responsibility leads to decreased helping**

Where people are in a group with a leader, group members believe that the leader should be the one to act. Suppose you are in a classroom and the fire alarm sounds. Would you stand up and shout "fire" or wait until the teacher, who has the responsibility for the class, gives the instruction to leave?

box. These participants were much more likely to offer help to an accomplice of Isen and Levin than were participants who had not found money. However, our assumption that being in a good mood increases the chances of helping is not necessarily true. In fact, positive emotions can help or hinder pro-social behaviour. Isen (1984), for example, suggests that people in a good mood are especially likely to recall pleasant memories. If the focus is on the bright side of life then optimistic feelings could well result in optimistic behaviour. However, through her further work, Isen suggests that sometimes happy people do not want to spoil their good mood by helping. Helping others may involve some cost and this may spoil the good mood.

On the other hand, we might think that being in a bad mood decreases the chances of helping. Evidence shows that negative emotions can lead to more, or less, pro-social behaviour. Two factors may determine this:

1 the mood itself and our personality: if helping others results in our feeling good about ourselves it can improve our bad mood. If, on the other hand, our helping someone will not make us feel good then we are less likely to offer help to a person in need.
2 our age: Cialdini et al. (1976) had participants of various ages think of either neutral or depressing events before being given the opportunity to donate. Results showed the younger participants donated less after thinking about depressing events whereas in older participants the difference was reversed, showing that some people remove a negatively induced mood by behaving more pro-socially.

Characteristics of those in need

Do we decide whether to help because of the type of person we are or because of the type of person the victim appears to be? Undoubtedly, we perceive that certain types of people are more deserving of help than others. We are more likely to help family and those to whom we are related and those for whom we are responsible. For example, in 1995 headteacher Philip Lawrence went to the aid of one of his pupils who was being bullied by youths from another school. One attacker stabbed Philip Lawrence who died from the wounds inflicted.

More generally:

- We are likely to help those who are physically similar to ourselves and who appear to share the same opinions and beliefs as ourselves. For example, a student is more likely to help another person who also appears to be a student.
- We are likely to help those we perceive as needing help: children, the elderly, people with pushchairs, the disabled.
- We are more likely to help those to whom we are physically attracted, as confirmed in studies by West and Brown (1975) for example.
- Studies have shown that we are less likely to help those who are not attractive, particularly those who are disfigured (unless we are also disfigured). Piliavin et al. (1981) found we are less likely to help a person who has a visible birthmark. Samerotte and Harris (1976) found that a person with a bandaged arm received most help, one with no bandage next and a person with a scar, eye-patch and bandage received the least help. One interpretation of the Samerotte and Harris study is that in the first condition the man is perceived as not being responsible for his condition as he has only a bandaged arm. In the last condition, as he has an eye-patch, and a scar in addition to the bandaged arm, he is responsible for his condition, could well be dangerous and should be avoided.
- Research on the race of the victim has produced mixed results. Gaertner and Dovidio (1977) staged an experiment similar to 'the lady in distress' study by Latané and Darley (1970), detailed later, where a lady fell off a chair in another room. In this study participants, who were all white, are shown a photograph of Brenda with whom the participants would be working – but they were to

work in different rooms. For some participants Brenda was 'white' and for others she was 'black'. Another variable is when participants were alone or when they were in groups. Brenda then worked from an adjacent room and at a prearranged time stacked chairs fell on her and she called for help. The results showed no racial discrimination at all; in fact slightly more of the 'white' participants helped when Brenda was 'black'.

Progress exercise

List three characteristics of people we are more likely to help.

List three characteristics of people we are less likely to help.

Gender and cultural differences in pro-social behaviour

Introduction

A common-sense view is that the relationship between men and women results in three levels of helping: that men are most likely to help a woman; that men–men and woman–woman helping is next; with women helping men the least. Whilst there is some evidence that this is true, the relationship is a little more complex because there are different types of helping. Generally, in Western cultures men are traditionally supposed to be chivalrous and heroic whereas the female role is more of long-term caring.

Gender differences

Is a man more likely to help a woman than vice versa? A number of studies have shown that this is true. In one variation of their studies involving drivers and hitchhikers, Pomazal and Clore (1973) found that male drivers were much more likely to stop for a woman than for a man. In a study which seemingly placed women in a potentially dangerous situation, Przybyla (1985) showed male participants sexually explicit videotapes and then noted whether they were more likely to help a male or female needing help. As might be expected, they were much more likely to help the woman. On the other hand, when female participants were shown sexually explicit videotapes they spent less time helping anyone, whether it be a male or female needing help.

In an extensive review of more than 170 studies, Eagly and Crowley (1986) concluded that there are gender differences in helping but that the difference is due to the application of traditional gender roles. Men are indeed more likely to help than women but only where brief, heroic, chivalrous acts are required. Men are far less likely to help, and this is where women dominate, in long-term, caring or nurturing situations which involve more commitment but less danger.

Cultural differences

Are people in all cultures socialised to help one another? Is altruism prized everywhere? A number of authors have attempted to answer these questions and have examined cross-cultural research, coming to the same broad conclusion that there are 'individualist' cultures and 'collectivist' cultures. Nobles (1976), for example, believes that **individualist cultures**, such as some European countries, the USA, Canada and Australia, are based on a world view emphasising individuality, uniqueness, difference and competition. **Collectivist cultures**, which include African and some Asian countries, are based on groupness, sameness, commonality and co-operation. As a result, collectivist cultures tend to be far more pro-social than others. This view is confirmed in a study of 134 children aged 3–10 years in 6 different cultures: India, Kenya, Okinawa, Mexico, the Philippines and the United States. The cultures in which children were more altruistic were the less industrialised (Whiting and Whiting 1975). Despite this there are individual variations amongst certain peoples, as found by field research.

Field research

The answer to the question posed above becomes more apparent when the following two examples are considered. At one extreme are the American-Indian cultures, which traditionally offer hospitality to every stranger, and at the other is an African mountain tribes-people known as the Ik. The following account of the Ik is provided by anthropologist Turnbull who writes, 'The people were as unfriendly, uncharitable, inhospitable and generally mean as any people can be. If when out walking I stumbled during a difficult descent . . . the Ik shrieked with laughter.' The Ik seemingly represent a society in which the total absence of pro-social behaviours has a survival value. In fact the Ik will steal, deceive or even kill one another to ensure their own survival.

In-group and out-group behaviour

Cultural differences play a major role in defining in-groups and out-groups. An in-group is the group with which an individual feels he or she is a member whereas the out-group is a group with which an individual does not identify. In interdependent or collectivist cultures greater emphasis is placed on co-operation and so members of such cultures are more likely to help in-group members than independent or individualistic cultures. Such findings have been found by a number of authors, such as Moghaddam, et al. (1993). Conversely, because of their collectivist nature, such cultures are less likely to help out-group members than are individualistic cultures (Triandis 1994), for example. It is not quite this simple and the following study shows that it is very difficult to isolate and measure a single variable. Feldman in 1968 conducted field studies in Boston, Paris and Athens. In each city he compared responses to a native and a non-native in a variety of situations such as asking for directions, overpaying a cashier, asking a resident if he/she had dropped some money, etc. In all, about 3,000 instances were recorded. Feldman found that for some of the situations there was no difference at all between the treatment of the native and the non-native. In others, however, he found that in Paris and Boston the non-native was treated better than the native whereas in Athens the native was treated better than the non-native. Feldman concluded, however, that the difference was not due to culture but simply due to the similarity of the person asking for help and the person giving it.

Situational determinants of helping behaviour

City versus rural life

City life is often anonymous and people are often nothing more than faces in the crowd. They do not have much contact with people whom they know and so they are less likely to give help to a person they do not know. In a rural village, however, where people may well know all others, people are much more likely to help. The two aspects to consider are: helping in a non-emergency situation and helping in an apparent emergency. Considering the former, is it true that people in cities are less likely to help than people from towns and villages? Suppose you knocked on a door explaining that you were visiting a friend and that you had lost the address. You still had the number and could you possibly use their 'phone to call your friend. Do you think that people would let you in? (Remember that mobile 'phones did not exist at this time!) Do you think it would make a difference if you were a man or woman? This situation is exactly the same as that created by Altman (1969). In her study she found that a woman was admitted to about 94 per cent of the small-town homes but only to 40 per cent of the city homes; a man was admitted to about 40 per cent of the small-town homes but only 14 per cent of the city homes (see Figure 4.2).

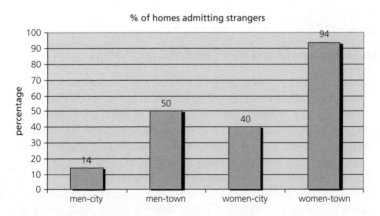

Figure 4.2 **Percentage of homes admitting a male or female stranger in a town compared to a city**

The stimulus overload theory

Milgram in 1970 extended the city *versus* rural debate when he proposed an explanation of why city people help less in emergency situations. Milgram proposed a **stimulus overload theory** suggesting that people from cities are so familiar with emergency situations that they become an everyday occurrence; consequently they are less likely to attract interest and so people do not help. On the other hand, those from relatively small towns do not witness emergency situations very often so when they occur their novelty is more likely to attract attention and help. This finding was confirmed in a study by Amato (1983), who, in 55 different Australian communities, examined a diverse range of behaviours such as a person dropping an envelope and observing whether passers-by would pick it up and return it. In another variation a man limped down a street then screamed, fell over and clutched his leg, which began bleeding profusely. When this study was carried out in a small town (of less than 1,000 inhabitants) about 50 per cent of witnesses who observed the incident stopped to help, whereas in a city of 20,000 to 30,000 this dropped to 25 per cent, with down to only 15 per cent of witnesses stopping to help in major cities of more than one million inhabitants. These findings have been confirmed in studies carried out around the world – in countries such as Israel, Turkey, the Sudan, Australia and Britain. The study is not ethical by today's standards, since participants were deceived: the man was an actor and the blood from the leg was not real.

Pro-social behaviour and environmental psychology

Environmental psychology is concerned with the way in which we interact with the environment. It influences us and we modify it in most things we do. A long-standing debate is whether **environmental determinism** governs all of our behaviour, whether it has a strong influence (known as **environmental probabilism**), whether it has some influence (**environmental possibilism**) or whether it has no influence at all on what we do (giving us **freedom**).

In relation to helping behaviour, environmental psychologists have looked at the effects of environmental factors such as odour, noise, crowding and temperature. Some of these factors increase the incidence of helping whilst some decrease it.

Pleasant odours

In a study carried out in the United States it was discovered that pleasant odours affect helping behaviour. Baron (1997) asked people to give him change for a $1 note – and if they stopped and changed the note he classed this as helping behaviour. His independent variables were various types of shop producing distinctive smells and these included a bakery, a coffee shop and a cookie store. For controls he used shops that did not produce pleasant odours, such as a news-agents. Baron found that pleasant odours do affect helping behaviour because 57 per cent helped when he was outside a shop emitting a pleasant odour compared with only 19 per cent when the odour was neutral.

Noise

Whereas pleasant odours result in increased helping, there are factors which lead to a decrease in helping. Two such factors are noise and crowding. Noise, defined simply as 'unwanted sound', has a negative effect on helping. To demonstrate this Mathews and Canon (1975) performed two studies, one in a laboratory and the other in the field. In the laboratory study participants sat in a waiting room with a confederate of the experimenter. Whilst waiting the participant was exposed to one of three conditions: 48 decibels of normal, background noise, 65dB of white noise or 85dB of white noise. During the noise the confederate got up and accidentally dropped a pile of books and papers. Whereas 72 per cent of participants helped in the 'normal noise' condition this reduced to 67 per cent with 65dB and to only 37 per cent offering help when the noise level was at 85dB.

In their field study a confederate of Mathews and Canon got out of a car as the participant was passing and again dropped books and papers. The background noise this time was 50db and the loud noise, created by a faulty lawnmower, was at 87dB. Mathews and Canon found that, in this study too, helping behaviour decreased when there was a loud noise.

Evaluation

Critics will, of course, point out that noise creates a 'narrowing of attention' and may result in the participant not even noticing that the confederate dropped the books; people also tend to walk faster to avoid such a noise and this explains the reduction in helping behaviour. To resolve this Page (1977) performed a study which had many similarities with the studies by Mathews and Canon but, instead of the confederate behaving passively, Page's confederate approached the participants directly and asked for help. The results of the study by Page confirm the conclusion that noise decreases willingness to help.

Density and crowding

Another environmental factor that affects helping behaviour is physical density. This is of two types: spatial density involves the size of an area such as a room and social density refers to the number of people in a given area. In field studies involving thirty six American cities Levine and colleagues (1994) found that the greater the social density the less likely people were to help. Crowding on the other hand is a psychological state involving feelings of restrictedness in limited spatial conditions. In a study in a cafeteria by Jorgensen and Dukes (1976) it was found that where the social density was high (i.e. when there were many people present) fewer people complied with a notice to return their trays. They also found that where social density was low more people helped by returning their trays to a designated area.

Temperature

We have seen that whilst some environmental factors affect helping positively, such as pleasant odours, some affect it negatively, such as noise and crowding. A final factor to consider is the effect of temperature on helping behaviour. The evidence is inconclusive and more research is needed. For example, whereas in 1978 a study by Page found that participants were much less likely to offer help when leaving an uncomfortably hot laboratory, studies by Schneider et al. (1980) found that heat had no effect on levels of helping. In a naturalistic study Cunningham (1979) found that outside temperature had no effect on the number of tips left by patrons of an indoor restaurant.

Progress exercise

List three characteristics of people we are more likely to help.

List three environmental factors which are likely to lead to less helping

Summary

In this chapter characteristics of the potential helper have been considered, including personality, religious beliefs, possession of appropriate skills and mood. The characteristics of those in need have also been considered. City life, a situational factor, is likely to lead to less helping than rural life. This may be due to stimulus overload. Both gender and cultural differences have been considered and both laboratory and field studies have provided evidence. Finally, studies from environmental psychology show that, whereas pleasant odours are likely to lead to more helping, we are less likely to help when the temperature is too high, it is noisy or when we feel crowded.

Review exercise

1. Suggest *two* methodological and/or ethical criticisms of at least two pieces of empirical research described in this chapter.
2. Discuss the view that the environment *determines* whether we help a person in need or not.

Further reading

Bell, P. A. et al. (1996) *Environmental Psychology* 4th edn, Orlando, FL: Harcourt Brace. General text on environmental psychology but excellent sections on environmental psychology and social behaviour.

Moghaddam, F.M. (1998) *Social Psychology: Exploring Universals across Cultures*. New York: W.H. Freeman. Excellent on cultural differences in pro-social behaviour.

Turnbull, C.M. (1972) *The Mountain People*. New York: Simon & Schuster. More details of the Ik.

5

Bystander effects on pro-social behaviour

Bystander effects in the laboratory
Explaining bystander effects in the laboratory
Bystander effects in the natural environment
Summary

In the Kitty Genovese incident (see Chapter 1) there were thirty-eight witnesses, yet no one helped or called the police. Theories such as those mentioned in Chapter 3 apply to the cognitive processes of an individual, and indeed it is likely that many of the witnesses would have been thinking about whether or not to help. However, probably the most important factor in explaining their inaction was the belief that someone else would help or call the police. The belief that others will help is crucial and so has been investigated in detail by psychologists.

Bystander effects in the laboratory

The Darley and Latané studies

In 1970 Latané and Darley conducted a series of laboratory studies to examine the influence of the presence of other people on helping behaviour. In one study, which they called 'a lady in distress', male students arrived to participate in a study and whilst in a waiting room they completed questionnaires about market research. From an adjoining room, they heard a woman first fall off her chair and then call out for help. 'Oh my God, my foot ... I ... can't move ... it. Oh my ankle ... I ... can't get this ... thing ... off me.' It was found that where there was only a single participant (*n*=26) *all* of the students responded with an offer to help, but in the condition where other students were present fewer than 62 per cent went to her aid. Darley and Latané thus concluded that the presence of other bystanders inhibited willingness to help. Similarly in a second study, their 'epileptic seizure' study, Darley and Latané (1968) had male students, again seated in a waiting room, hear a person in an adjoining room having an epileptic fit. The results of this study are shown in Table 5.1.

Two conclusions can be drawn from this data: as the number of bystanders increased, the percentage of participants who helped during the fit decreased; as the number of bystanders increased the participants took longer to help. This data left Latané and Darley in no doubt that individuals are less likely to help when they are in the presence of others.

Table 5.1 **Percentage of participants helping the victim of an epileptic fit**

Group size	Total number of participants studied	% responding during fit	% responding at any point	Average response time (in seconds)
1	13	85	100	52
2	26	62	85	93
5	13	31	62	166

Source: Adapted from Latané and Darley 1970

Evaluation

These studies are limited in many ways and should not be generalised. They involved only male students who were all American and they knew that they were taking part in a laboratory experiment. The participants were also deceived because they thought they were waiting for a study to begin and, of course, the events of the fall and seizure were faked.

Further Darley and Latané studies

These limitations did not stop Darley and Latané in their quest for answers. They wondered, if people would not help others in emergencies would they help themselves? Darley and Latané (1968) performed another study, the 'smoke-filled room experiment'. In this study whilst participants, male students at Columbia University, are in the waiting room to discuss some of the problems involved in an urban university, it begins to fill with smoke. This continues until the room is full of thick, white smoke or until a participant takes action. In the condition where participants were alone, 75 per cent of the twenty-four tested walked out of the room to report the problem. Apparently there was no panic and most participants simply said, 'There's something strange going on in there, there seems to be some sort of smoke coming through the wall.' In the condition where two experimenter accomplices were present with the participant, of all those tested, only one participant took any action. The other participants continued 'doggedly working on their questionnaires and waving the fumes away from their faces. They coughed, rubbed their eyes and opened a window – but they did not report the smoke' (52).

This result confirms the powerful effect of bystanders, at least in an experimental situation. When Latané and Darley asked participants about their inaction, several thought the smoke was smog designed to simulate an urban environment and two participants thought it was a truth gas so they would answer the questionnaires correctly!

Progress exercise

Outline three advantages and three disadvantages of conducting psychological research in a laboratory

Explaining bystander effects in the laboratory

As found in studies such as those detailed above, most participants do not help either themselves or others. A number of reasons have been proposed to explain the influence of bystanders on helping.

Audience inhibition

When competent people have an audience (the bystanders) their performance improves. This is known as the **social facilitation effect**. However, when people are less competent their performance is worse when carried out in front of an audience than when performed alone. Consider how **audience inhibition** would apply in the study by Cramer et al. (1988) (see Chapter 4, p. 43) where nurses were compared with students. A nurse (in theory) would know how to assist a person with a medical problem whereas the average (non-medical) student would not and so tend to do nothing. Audience inhibition suggests that if we do not think we are competent then we do nothing when others who are present also do nothing. Further, individuals who fear embarrassment are less likely to draw attention to themselves if there is any possibility that the situation may not be an emergency. You may also recall the findings of the Staub (1979) study (see Chapter 2, p. 20) where older children are less likely to help another child in distress because they fear criticism from an adult.

Diffusion of responsibility

When only one person is in attendance at a particular event then that person is 100 per cent responsible for giving help. Where there are two people then responsibility is divided (i.e. each person is 50 per cent responsible). If there are ten bystanders then the onus of responsibility is diffused amongst all ten. This can easily explain the Kitty Genovese case where witnesses assumed that someone else had 'phoned for the police. Support for the notion of diffusion of responsibility comes not only from the Latané and Darley studies, but also from *social loafing* research where it has been demonstrated that the more people there are present, the less effort each individual applies.

Pluralistic ignorance

In making a decision whether or not to help, one important clue for a person's action (or inaction) is to consider what the other bystanders are doing. As an emergency situation may be ambiguous, it is logical for us to wait for further developments and the most obvious clue is to see if other people help. If one person defines the situation as an emergency and springs into action we are likely to follow and give assistance. If no one moves to help then we conclude that it cannot be an emergency and so we do nothing. In effect, each bystander looks to the behaviour of others as a guide to his or her own behaviour. In the smoke-filled room experiment participants made social comparisons, saw everyone else appearing to be undisturbed by the smoke and so defined the situation as a non-emergency. In the Kitty Genovese case, since no one was seen to be intervening, this tended to define the situation as one not requiring intervention from anyone else.

Briefly describe what is meant by the terms audience inhibition, diffusion of responsibility, pluralistic ignorance.

Progress exercise

To provide support for their interpretation, Latané and Darley (1976) performed a complex study which involved a number of conditions designed to test diffusion of responsibility and audience inhibition. In the study, participants arrive, supposedly to take part in an experiment on aggression which involves the use of an electric shock generator. The emergency is created when the experimenter receives a violent shock from the unreliable generator and is thrown against a wall. Using television cameras and monitors wired to different participants' rooms the participants are allocated to one of five conditions (see Table 5.2).

According to Latané and Darley the person receiving the electric shock should be helped most by those who are in the control group as they are not influenced by others and they are solely responsible for helping. As participants become more aware of the presence of others (diffusion of responsibility) there should be less helping and as others become more aware of the participants (audience inhibition and social influence) there should be less helping still. This is exactly what the results of the study showed with a cumulative effect as each factor was added to the next.

Evaluation

Whilst it is entirely logical to take a real-life event (the Kitty Genovese incident) into a laboratory to try to find an explanation for it (such as in the Latané and Darley studies), laboratory studies have a number of inherent weaknesses, such as low **ecological validity** and **demand characteristics**. The Latané and Darley studies also break many ethical guidelines: participants in the 1976 study did not give informed consent as they thought it was a study about aggression; they were deceived as the experimenter did not actually receive an electric shock; and they may have been upset by the potentially tragic consequences of the event.

Other studies have been designed to explain the effect of bystanders and many have been performed in the natural environment.

Bystander effects in the natural environment

Introduction

In 1975 Latané and Dabbs performed a study where a person in a lift dropped some books. They found that the probability of receiving

Table 5.2 Design for audience inhibition and diffusion of responsibility

	Participant's room	Other participant's room
1. The control group: the participant cannot see others and others cannot see them	camera aimed at ceiling	monitor shows ceiling
2. Diffusion of responsibility: the participant knows there is another participant but cannot see or hear him	camera aimed at ceiling	monitor shows ceiling
3. Diffusion and social influence: the participant can see the other participant but knows the other participant cannot see	camera aimed at ceiling	monitor shows other participant
4. Diffusion and audience inhibition: the participant cannot see the other participant but knows the other participant can see him	camera aimed at participant	monitor shows ceiling
5. Diffusion and audience inhibition and social influence: the participant can see the other participant and knows that the other participant can see him	camera aimed at participant	monitor shows other participant

Source: Adapted from Latané and Darley 1976

help decreased as the number of people present increased: 40 per cent helped when one other passenger was present but only 15 per cent helped when there were six others. However, not all studies carried out in a natural environment have found that large numbers of bystanders mean less willingness to help.

Subway Samaritans

Piliavin, Rodin and Piliavin (1969) conducted a study to investigate the effects on helping behaviour of the type of person who is in need. Two 'victim' variables were examined: the first involved an 'ill/drunk' victim, in which one member of the team would either carry a cane (ill condition) or appear drunk (drunk condition), and the second was based on the ethnicity of the victim ('black' or 'white').

During the seven and a half-minutes' journey on a New York subway train the 'victim', at a prearranged time, collapsed on the floor of the train and remained there until someone helped. The major findings of the study were as follows:

1 Those appearing to be ill were more likely to be helped than those appearing to be drunk (in the ill condition, 62 helping responses were observed out of 65 trials; in the drunk condition there were 19 responses out of 38 trials).
2 The ethnicity of the 'victim' had little effect on the helper.
3 The expected diffusion of responsibility effect, which Piliavin et al. had assumed would also apply following the results of the Latané and Darley laboratory studies, did not occur. Why was this? It is suggested by Piliavin et. al. that in the laboratory studies participants could *hear* but not *see* the 'victim', whereas in their study participants could both see and hear the 'victim'. Piliavin et al. believe that this face-to-face contact negates diffusion of responsibility.

Piliavin et al. conclude that the most appropriate explanation for the helping behaviour observed in their study is a combination of emotional arousal and cost–benefit analysis, both of which were described earlier (see Chapter 3).

Evaluation

Although there are advantages to carrying out a study in the natural environment, such as high ecological validity, there are also problems. Consider the ethics of the Piliavin et al. study. Participants:

- did not give their consent to participate;
- could not withdraw from the situation;
- were deceived as the 'victim' did not really need help;
- may well have suffered psychological harm: they may have become upset by a person collapsing before their eyes.

The study also included a number of design flaws, such as the fact that all of the 'victims' were male and that there was a marked imbalance between the number of trials for the 'ill' compared to 'drunk' conditions: some 65 trials for the former, compared to 38 for the latter, simply because the students 'didn't like playing the drunk!'

In a damning criticism of experimental studies such as those above that try to explain events such as the Kitty Genovese incident, Banyard and Grayson (1996) suggest that the experimenters 'seem to have gone to the theatre and described the audience without ever looking at the play' (15). By this they mean that the focus of attention is always on the behaviour of the bystanders when surely it should be on the perpetrator, the person committing the crime. Thus in the Kitty Genovese incident the focus of attention should have been not only on the thirty-eight witnesses but also on Walter Moseley who had murdered three other women and raped at least four more.

Outline three advantages and three disadvantages of conducting psychological research in a natural environment.

Progress exercise

Summary

A significant number of studies in psychology consider what people do as individuals without looking at what effect being with friends, family, work colleagues, or even strangers would have. In this chapter the effect of the presence of other people has been examined. Generally, laboratory studies have shown that people are less likely to help when other people are present. This is explained through audience inhibition, diffusion of responsibility and pluralistic ignorance. However, in contrast to the above, naturalistic studies have shown that people help and the diffusion of responsibility group of explanations does not apply. Piliavin et al. suggest the difference can be explained because in the laboratory participants were not face-to-face with the victim whereas in the field studies they were.

Review exercise

Essay question: Critically assess psychological studies conducted on the effect of bystander behaviour.

Further reading

Latané, B. and Darley, J.M. (1970) *The Unresponsive Bystander: Why Doesn't He Help*. New York: Appleton Century Crofts. (The original publication including most of the laboratory bystander studies.)

Section II

ANTI-SOCIAL BEHAVIOUR

6

Traditional explanations of anti-social behaviour

 Instinct theories of anti-social behaviour
Social learning and aggression
Summary

Instinct theories of anti-social behaviour

A number of psychologists believe that aggression is instinctive, that humans have an innate need to behave aggressively.

Freud on aggression

Freud's first view on aggression, as it was not part of his original theory of psychosexual development, was outlined in a famous letter he wrote to Albert Einstein in 1932. Einstein had asked Freud how to protect mankind from the atrocities of the First World War. In the letter Freud stated that aggression has a biological basis. He believed that human behaviour is driven by two instincts: Eros, the life instinct, and Thanatos, the death instinct. As these two instincts are in conflict the energy produced is displaced to the 'real world' and aggression acts as a safety valve to dissipate the energy. This means that aggression need not be destructive; indeed, for the individual releasing it, it is very constructive. Freud's approach (and also that of Lorenz, see p. 70) are said to be hydraulic – the pressure builds up and unless it is allowed to be released it will produce some sort of damage. For Freud the aggressive energy built up between the two instincts must be released and any outlet will be sufficient. One *constructive* outlet is to channel the aggressive energy into sport; another outlet, which is *destructive*, is any form of anti-social aggression. A further implication is that the build-up and release of aggression is inevitable and *must* happen in everyone without exception and it *must* happen throughout life. Despite this there is no substantial research showing that people have built-in, uncontrollable urges to fight and kill. Moreover, the evidence suggests that expressing aggression does not always reduce aggressiveness, as Freud predicted.

Lorenz on aggression

In his 1966 book, Lorenz defined aggression as 'the fighting instinct in beast and man which is directed against members of the same species'. Lorenz believed therefore that aggression is innate and genetically programmed into both humans and other animals. He believed it is genetic because aggression is necessary for the survival of a species. Although this definition refers to members of the same species, there are two types of aggression: **intra-species aggression**, which is between two members of the same species, and **inter-species aggression**, which is between two different species.

The purpose of intra-species aggression is to keep members of the same species apart so each has enough territory and therefore sufficient resources to survive. More than this, intra-species aggression allows sexual selection of the strongest and best mate to continue the species. Notably, intra-species aggression usually ends in appeasement by the loser rather than death. Lorenz believes that this is because animals that are fierce predators, and have the ability to kill relatively easily, all have biological inhibiting mechanisms which prevent them from destroying members of their own species. Most conflicts between animals involve **threat displays** which are an attempt to assert authority without actually inflicting harm. For example, some animals such as lizards threaten by making themselves appear larger; others such as baboons bare their teeth. When fighting does occur it is often **ritualised**, which means it is conducted as if it were some kind of tournament with a fixed set of rules where the participants are not allowed to inflict serious damage. The result of the challenge will often end with an **appeasement gesture** where one animal adopts a submissive posture indicating that it has admitted defeat. Such a display is evident in dogs which roll on their back. At this point the fighting stops and the dominant animal does not go in for the kill, according to Lorenz because of the inhibiting mechanism.

Inter-species aggression is where one species kills another for food and, although there is a clear attempt to harm, it is not done in response to anger and there is no intent to cause suffering. The drive which the animal needs to satisfy is hunger and not aggression. As Lorenz puts it, the dog that is on the verge of catching a rabbit never growls nor does it have its ears laid back. This predatory aggression is species-specific. It has even been discovered that in the cat predatory aggression such as stalking a rat and aggression as an act of self-defence are controlled by two different areas of the hypothalamus.

Within human evolution the inhibiting mechanism or safety device did not evolve because we are not equipped with natural weapons: humans can rarely kill each other with a single blow. The advent of weapons provided a means of inflicting considerable damage on others without any innate inhibitions. Some people argue that the use of weapons is uniquely human (although chimpanzees sometimes use weapons). However, it is argued that in humans fighting represents the failure of threat displays.

Evaluation

The views of Lorenz have been criticised in a number of ways. His idea that non-human animals do not kill members of their own species is incorrect – infanticide is one of the most common forms of aggression amongst animals. Others suggest his explanations of aggression are little more than loose comparisons between human and animal behaviour, that human behaviour is much more complex and that his analysis of animal behaviour itself is wrong. Of course, if aggression were instinctual or biologically pre-programmed all societies would be equally aggressive and clearly they are not.

Summarise Freud's theory of aggression and compare with Lorenz's theory of aggression.

Social learning and aggression

Introduction

According to social learning theorists, although the aggressive behaviour of lower animals may be explained in terms of instinctual drives, aggression in humans is a learned behaviour. How does this learning take place? Two processes are at work:

1 **Imitation** where a child who sees a model behaving in a particular way is likely to reproduce that behaviour.
2 **Reinforcement** based originally on Thorndike's law of effect which states that 'behaviours that are rewarded (positively reinforced) tend to be repeated and behaviours that are not rewarded (negatively reinforced) tend not to be repeated'. The role of punishment also plays a major role in the process.

Both of these processes can be seen in everyday life, such as when a child uses aggression to take a toy away from another child. If the child goes unchallenged about its action the child learns that the aggression produced the desired reward. Another demonstration is when a toddler, who is learning to walk, collides with a chair and falls over, and a parent then tells the child to 'smack the naughty chair'.

Laboratory studies of imitation and reinforcement

Both imitation and reinforcement have been demonstrated in the laboratory by studies conducted by Bandura and colleagues. The first study demonstrates imitation.

Bandura, Ross and Ross (1961) used 36 boys and 36 girls (37–69 months; mean age 52 months) from Stanford University nursery school as participants. The two main groups were those who would observe a model behave aggressively and those who would not. Crucially, to control for any pre-existing aggression, the groups were matched for aggression before the study. (Each was rated on four different five-point scales by an experimenter and the nursery-school teacher but not the parent!) The children were also matched with same-sex and opposite-sex models (female child with same sex and opposite sex; male child with same and opposite sex). The procedure involved all children being taken individually to a room that had a number of toys, including a 5-foot inflatable Bobo doll. Children in the non-aggressive groups saw the adult model play with the toys but ignore the Bobo doll. Children in the 'aggressive' groups saw the model perform both physically aggressive actions against the Bobo doll (sits on it and punches it in the nose, etc.) and verbally aggressive actions (model says 'pow' and 'punch him in the nose'). After this the children were taken to another room where they were subjected to mild frustration: they saw some toys but were not allowed to play with them. They were then taken to the next room where there were some toys, including a 3-foot Bobo doll (the right size for children) and left alone. The experimenters observe their actions through a one-way mirror.

A number of conclusions can be drawn from the results:

- children who observed the aggressive model behaved more aggressively than children who did not;
- boys made more aggressive acts than did girls;
- the boys showed more aggression if the model was male;
- the girls showed more physical aggression if the model was male but more verbal aggression if the model was female;
- children imitated specific acts.

If a child learns by imitation, as demonstrated above, then such learning is likely to be repeated if the behaviour is *positively reinforced*. This is Thorndike's principle which states that any behaviour that is positively reinforced is likely to be repeated in the future, whilst behaviour either not rewarded, or punished is less likely to be repeated. This was shown in another study by Bandura.

Bandura (1965) divided sixty-six nursery-school children into three groups. All three groups watched a film where an adult model kicked and punched a Bobo doll:

- condition 1: the children saw the adult model being rewarded by a second adult.
- condition 2: the children saw a second adult telling off the adult model for the aggressive behaviour.
- condition 3: the adult model was neither rewarded nor punished.

The children were then allowed to play in the room with the Bobo doll whilst the experimenters watched through a one-way mirror. The results showed that children in all three groups imitated the aggressive behaviour, and those in the model-reward condition were especially likely to repeat the behaviour.

Evaluation

A few years later Bandura (1977) looked again at his initial work and distinguished between learning and performance because, although children may have learned aggression, they also learn when it is (such as the model-reward condition) and when it is not appropriate to behave in this way (such as in the model-punished condition). Therefore, just because a behaviour is learned, it does not mean it will automatically be performed.

Progress exercise

Use your imagination here: how many things have you learned (things that you know how to do) but would never dream of performing. List ten examples – if you dare!

What is important is to look at the situations and circumstances in which a person will perform a learned behaviour. For example, it has been found that the type of role model is crucial and studies have shown that the more important, successful, powerful and liked the role model is, the more likely that person is to be imitated. Initially, a child's parents fulfil all these criteria. Later on, a child's peers become influential models.

Critics of the Bandura studies point out that the studies don't really involve aggression – some people say it is only true aggression if it is directed at another living being. We could accept this if we define aggression very narrowly but it would mean, for example, that a person who smashes items in her home, possibly destroying them, is not behaving aggressively.

Another criticism aimed at the Bandura studies is that children who observe aggression and imitate it in a laboratory setting will not generalise such behaviour to real-life settings. This criticism is common for many laboratory studies. However, it is clear, as will be seen below, that children do observe and imitate in the real world just as they do in the laboratory and that this is true for adults too.

Three other points are worth considering:

1 If children imitate models, what is the role of the media: to what extent does television violence influence the behaviour of children – and adults too for that matter?
2 Adults play a major role as models for their children. In relation to aggression Sears et al. (1957) amongst others have found that parents who are aggressive tend to produce children who are aggressive themselves. Punishment at home often works but children who are punished severely at home tend to be more aggressive outside the home. More details of this appear in Chapter 9 where punishment as a means of controlling aggression is considered.
3 Bandura has revised his own views. Whereas initially he considered imitation to be important, he now considers that there is much more to observational learning and has developed this into social cognitive theory.

Cultural diversity and learning

Although Bandura would argue that the processes involved in the learning of any behaviour (and not just aggression) are universal, he would agree that different environmental factors would have an effect on the behaviour of those exposed to such factors. One important factor is the way in which different cultures allow the expression of aggression. Osterwell and Nagano-Nakamura (1992) have shown that whereas Israeli mothers believe aggression should be expressed outside the family, Japanese mothers believe it should be expressed within the family. It has also been shown that when they were an ethnic minority in school, Hispanic children were more moody but tolerant of aggression whereas Anglo children were not more moody but more aggressive; this being attributed to differing cultural child-rearing practices.

Summary

This chapter introduces traditional explanations of anti-social behaviour. Such traditional theories locate the cause within the individual rather than the wider society. Reflecting the nature–nurture debate, the main opposing views are those who argue aggression is instinctive and those who argue that it is learned. Freud believed that aggression has a biological basis and that an outlet for instinctive energies is needed. Constructive aggression involves participation in sport and destructive aggression that includes any form of anti-social aggression. Lorenz argued that aggression was necessary for the survival of a species and, as survival is essential, it is instinctive. The social learning theorists believe that aggression in humans, like all other behaviour, is learned. The pioneer Bandura performed many studies in the 1960s which seemed to show that if children observe a behaviour they will imitate it. The effect becomes more pronounced if an aggressive act is rewarded or punished.

Review exercise

Describe two theories suggesting that anti-social behaviour is instinctive. Compare and contrast with evidence suggesting that anti-social behaviour is not instinctive.

Further reading

Krahe, B. (2001) *The Social Psychology of aggression*. Hove: Psychology Press. This text has good chapters on both of the 'traditional' approaches covered in this chapter.

7

Social-psychological explanations of anti-social behaviour

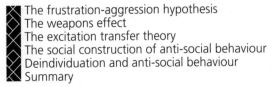

The frustration-aggression hypothesis
The weapons effect
The excitation transfer theory
The social construction of anti-social behaviour
Deindividuation and anti-social behaviour
Summary

Perhaps the most important theory to stimulate research on anti-social behaviour was that proposed some sixty years ago which suggested that frustration is a major cause of aggression. Frustration occurs when a person is prevented from achieving a goal; more formally, **frustration** is the blocking of goal-directed behaviour. This means that we might expect that whenever we are thwarted in our efforts to complete a task or achieve a goal, whatever that goal might be, we may become aggressive. In fact there are three factors that determine the amount of frustration we feel:

1 how strong the drive to achieve a goal is;
2 the number of frustrating incidents we experience;
3 whether the blocking of our goal is total or partial.

Progress exercise

Examples of frustration-aggression in real life are plentiful. List three or four instances where you were frustrated and where you may even have behaved aggressively.

However, we do not always vent our frustration on the object which caused it (we would look rather silly stamping on the filling of our sandwich which has fallen on to the floor) but our aggression may be delayed, it may be disguised or it may be displaced to a more acceptable outlet. For example, you are unlikely to behave aggressively to a teacher who has set yet another essay with a short deadline but you may well go home and (though hopefully not) kick your dog or flick your hamster!

The frustration-aggression hypothesis

In 1939 Dollard, Doob, Miller, Mowrer and Sears of Yale University formulated the frustration-aggression hypothesis. This had two assertions:

1 frustration *always* leads to some form of aggression and
2 aggression *always* stems from frustration.

This suggests, without exception, that frustration will result in aggression of some form and that aggression has no other cause but frustration.

Laboratory demonstrations of frustration and aggression

Does this hypothesis have any evidence to support it? One supporting study was performed by Barker et al. (1941). They had an experimental condition where young children were separated from desirable toys by a wire screen, allowing them to see the toys but not play with them.

After a long wait they were allowed to play with the toys. In a control condition children were allowed to play with the toys immediately without being frustrated. Barker et al. found that the frustrated group behaved aggressively by smashing the toys against the floor and the walls, by stamping on them and generally behaving destructively. This supports the frustration-aggression hypothesis as the non-frustrated group did not behave aggressively at all. In everyday life we are all likely to observe at some point someone lashing out at a person or object that has frustrated them. Frustration could be the cause of aggressive behaviour such as road and air rage.

Measuring aggression in the laboratory

How can aggression be measured? In children, studying aggression is relatively straightforward as one can simply observe and record aggressive behaviour, as in the Barker et al. study above. Bandura, for example, recorded the number of times a child punched or kicked a Bobo doll.

In laboratory studies involving adults, aggression is usually measured through the number, intensity or duration of electric shocks. This approach is typified by Buss (1963) who, in an attempt to measure aggression objectively, particularly the intensity of aggression, devised an **aggression machine**. This was simply an electric shock generator and in a typical study the participant would deliver an electric shock (or so they thought) to a victim, who was an accomplice of the experimenter. This technique is sometimes referred to as the **shock-learning technique**. A similar technique, often referred to as the **shock-competition technique**, has two participants in competition, each of whom gives electric shocks to the other.

Both these approaches suffer from a number of problems:

* ethics: they both rely on deceiving participants and so the participants cannot be giving fully informed consent. It may well be harmful to participants to think they have given another participant an electric shock. The opposite may well be argued, as with the Milgram obedience studies, that the value of the knowledge gained outweighs a few minor ethical transgressions;
* reality: such laboratory studies are subject to demand characteristics of the experimental situation and it is argued that participants know

they are taking part in a study and so refrain from venting their full aggressive impulse.

Despite the above problems, in 1963 Buss used his aggression machine to investigate how frustration related to aggression. Using three causes of frustration (task failure, interference with attempts to win money, and interference with getting a better course grade), Buss found that all three 'frustrated' groups gave more 'shocks' than a control group. However, Buss suggested that frustration and aggression might be linked only when aggression will quell the frustration and he suggested other variables, such as those considered below.

Variables affecting frustration-aggression

When the interruption of a goal is unexpected or when the interruption is perceived as illegitimate, as in the following study, aggression is said to increase. Kulik and Brown (1979) had students earn money by telephoning people (who were accomplices of the experimenter) to ask them for donations to a charity. The students were told to expect a high rate of contributions and so there was the potential for them to earn a large amount of money. When the students called and asked for a donation, all accomplices refused. Some accomplices were polite and gave reasonable explanations for not giving ('I can't afford to contribute'); others were insulting and gave no reason at all ('charities are a waste of time'). Kulik and Brown found that the students were apparently more frustrated by the latter response and used more aggressive language to those on the other end of the telephone, even venting their anger by slamming down the handset.

The closer people are to achieving a goal, the more frustration they will experience if they are thwarted or their progress towards it is interrupted. Support for this variable derives from a study by Harris (1974). In her study Harris asked a confederate to push in front of other people who were waiting in a queue. Sometimes the confederate pushed into the queue near the back (twelfth in line) and sometimes very near the front (after the second person). This was repeated in a number of different queues, such as a queue for cinema tickets and at a supermarket check-out. In her study Harris found that the responses of the people in the queue immediately behind the intruding confederate were much more aggressive when the confederate pushed in when they were near the front of the line than when they were near the back. This suggests that the closer a person is to achieving a goal, the more frustration they will experience when they are thwarted.

You have probably been in a situation where you are in a queue and somebody has pushed in. Were you frustrated? What did you do: quietly say nothing or punch the person on the nose? Suggest how your frustration and/or aggression could be measured in this situation.

Progress exercise

Frustration and anti-social behaviour

Frustration not only leads to aggression but can also lead to other forms of anti-social behaviour. In a study by Milgram and Shotland (1973) anti-social behaviour was measured by stealing money from a charity display. In this study they had more than 500 participants attend the *Network Television Preview Theatre* to watch a show and then give their opinion about it. For their trouble participants would receive a free transistor radio. After they had watched the show and answered the questions they were given a gift certificate and instructions to collect their radio from 'Bartel World Wide' at another location. Of course, this other location consisted of fake company offices with no one there, except for concealed video cameras to record the participants' behaviour. When the participants arrived at the office there was a poster advertising a charity display and a plastic container underneath containing a $10 note, some $1 notes and some coins. For half of them there was a sign that read, 'Notice – sorry to inconvenience you, but this office is temporarily closed because of illness. Kindly pick up your radio in room 1800 of this building.' This notice was intended to create mild frustration. The other half of the participants, the high-frustration group, saw a sign that read, 'Notice – we have no more transistor radios to distribute. We are closed until further notice.' Milgram and Shotland reasoned that the participants in the high-frustration group were more likely to steal the money than those in the low-frustration group. This is what they found:

only 2.9 per cent of participants in the low-frustration group stole the money compared to 18.7 per cent of those in the high-frustration group.

Evaluation

Despite experimental support for the frustration-aggression hypothesis there are limitations. Other studies have shown no link at all between frustration and aggression even when the frustration is strong, unexpected and illegitimate. In fact, very few psychologists now hold the view that frustration is the only cause of aggression and that aggressive behaviour inevitably follows when people are stopped from achieving their goals. Think about it: do you always respond with an aggressive action every time you are frustrated? Taking the first assertion of the frustration-aggression hypothesis, it is clear that frustration does not *always* lead to some form of aggression. People respond in many ways when they are frustrated, such as resigned acceptance, withdrawal, apathy and even increased efforts to achieve a goal. Because frustration does not always lead to aggression, Miller, one of the original research team and fully aware of this weakness in the theory, changed the first assertion to read 'frustration produces instigations to a number of different types of responses, one of which is an instigation to some form of aggression' (Barker et al. 1941: 337–338).

The second assertion is also flawed, for it is clear that not all aggression results from frustration. Consider the earlier definitions which outlined sanctioned aggression and pro-social aggression: neither involve frustration. Further, although people may well feel frustrated and come close to behaving aggressively, rather than acting without thinking, they stop to think about the appropriateness of their actions. Despite its limitations, the frustration-aggression hypothesis stimulated much research simply because psychologists wished to identify in which situations and in what circumstances frustration did lead to aggression. Such research will be considered in the next section.

Name two ways in which aggression has been measured in the laboratory. Suggest two ethical problems with such measures.

Progress exercise

The weapons effect

One of the most influential psychologists to reformulate the frustration-aggression hypothesis is Berkowitz who claimed that two factors are prerequisites of aggression:

1   a readiness to act aggressively, which is usually provided by frustration; and
2   external cues that trigger the expression of aggression.

This means that unless an external or situational influence suggests aggression to an individual they will not behave aggressively. The most obvious factor to suggest aggression is an actual weapon, which led to this being known as the weapons effect.

Initially, Berkowitz and LePage (1967) suggested that the mere availability of weapons increased aggression. If, for example, a person has a collection of guns, and guns have, according to Berkowitz, been associated with aggression on so many occasions that they become aggressive cues. As a result their mere presence may facilitate aggressive behaviour even if the guns themselves are not used aggressively. In the words of Berkowitz, 'guns not only permit violence, they can stimulate it as well. The finger pulls the trigger, but the trigger may also be pulling the finger' (1967: 22). Supporting the 'pure' Berkowitz view is a case reported in February 2000 where Allan Moynihan shot teenager Lee Hickman in the neck with an air rifle. Police found more than ten replica firearms including a submachine gun, a Kalashnikov rifle and a sawn-off shotgun at Moynihan's home.

PRO-SOCIAL AND ANTI-SOCIAL BEHAVIOUR

Laboratory demonstrations of the weapons effect

A number of laboratory studies carried out by Berkowitz and colleagues have successfully demonstrated the weapons effect. The usual procedure is to have a participant introduced to a confederate who then angers the participant in some way. After this the participant has the opportunity to behave aggressively to the confederate – usually through administering an electric shock. This format allowed a number of variables to be examined. In one study (Berkowitz and LePage, 1967) the confederate is introduced to the participant either as a boxer or as someone who has no aggressive associations. The participant delivered more severe shocks to the boxer. Another variation (also 1967) involved confederates being introduced as either *Kirk* Anderson or *Bob* Anderson. Participants then watched the aggressive film *Champion* about a prize-fight boxer (in which the boxer was played by *Kirk* Douglas) or a non-aggressive film. Participants were then either angered or not by the confederate. The results showed that participants gave more shocks when they were angered, and when they watched the aggressive film. And, surprising as it may seem, when the confederate was called Kirk, an average of 6.09 shocks were received compared to when the confederate was Bob, who only received 4.55 shocks.

In another variation, Berkowitz and LePage (1967) found participants exhibited more aggression when a shotgun and a revolver were displayed than when neutral objects (such as a badminton racquet) or no objects were displayed to participants. In yet another variation designed to show that the mere presence of weapons is important, participants were told either that the weapons were associated with the study or were totally unassociated. The results in Table 7.1 show there was very little difference between the number of shocks in the associated (6.07) and unassociated (5.67) conditions but a significant difference between these and a no-weapons condition (4.67).

Evaluation

The above-mentioned studies support the Berkowitz hypothesis that the mere presence of weapons facilitates aggressive behaviour. One evaluation issue is whether the results of these studies, where

Table 7.1 Electric shocks and the presence of weapons

	weapons present		no weapons present
	participants told weapons *associated* with study	participants told weapons *unassociated* with study	
Average no. of shocks	6.07	5.67	4.67

Berkowitz typically used male students at United States universities, can be generalised. In one variation, Frodi (1975) used Swedish high school students and found the same effect. Although the results were replicated in another country, the participants were still students. However, many other studies do not support the weapons effect. Page and Scheidt (1971) have suggested that it is not the mere presence of the weapons but the way the participants *interpret* the use of the weapons. It is also suggested that the results are due to demand characteristics and participants second-guess what the experiment is about. Only when the participants are totally naive, that is when they have no idea that the weapons may be part of the study, is the effect achieved. Of course, all of the studies are unethical in that they involve deception about the electric shock the participant has to administer to measure aggression. Finally, although Berkowitz is suggesting that 'the trigger can also pull the finger', at the end of the day a gun is an inanimate object that cannot fire by itself. A famous American slogan states 'guns don't kill people, people do'.

Weapons and cultural differences

Despite the contradictory findings research points to the dangers of having weapons freely available in society. In a cross-national study of violence in 1984, Archer and Gartner found that homicide rates in countries all over the world are highly correlated with the availability of handguns. Vancouver (Canada), for example, restricts handgun ownership whereas Seattle (United States) does not. The murder rate in Seattle is twice that of Vancouver. In Britain, where the use of guns is banned, the homicide rate is one-sixteenth that of the United States. However, just because high correlations have been found, cause and effect cannot be assumed.

Although the laboratory evidence of the weapons effect is ambiguous and often dismissed, the impact on a society cannot be ignored. The mere presence of weapons in society could well lead to a generally more aggressive society as suggested by the cross-national studies above. In support of this possibility, in a study comparing eleven countries, teenagers were asked to complete a story that involved conflict. Compared to all other countries the United States teenagers believed the conflict would end violently. As Archer (1994: 19) states, the United States teenagers were 'lethal, gun-laden and merciless'.

The effect of the wider use of weapons such as in a war also affects the behaviour of people in society. Archer and Gartner (1976) discovered that in nations that had been at war there was a dramatic increase in post-war homicide rates. Following World War II, compared to pre-war rates, France had an increase of 51 per cent, Italy 133 per cent and the Netherlands 13 per cent. Archer and Gartner also note that during the Vietnam War the murder rate in the United States more than doubled after a thirty-year decline. Apparently the war acted as a 'weapons effect'. War is sanctioned aggression and so it is interesting to see the effect this has on society as a whole.

The excitation transfer theory

Following the work of Schachter on the two-factor theory of emotion, which considers emotion to comprise both arousal and cognition, Zillmann (1988) in his **excitation transfer theory** argues similarly that arousal and cognition factors interact in shaping aggression. Zillman recognises that the arousal may be expressed in an aggressive manner immediately after an event but that this is not always possible. He suggests that when we are physiologically aroused, no matter what the cause, the arousal takes time to dissipate. This means that, although we may leave the situation that initially aroused us, the *excitation* remains with us and is *transferred* to another situation. When another event, which may be totally unrelated to the first, causes mild frustration or annoyance we may respond in a manner that is much more aggressive than we would usually exhibit or than the situation warrants.

Zillmann's theory can easily be applied to real-life events. In 1996 Stuart Hulse was at a party where the participants watched pornographic videotapes. Later he was left in a frustrated state of sexual arousal as participants paired off for sex. On his way home he found a victim whom he sexually attacked and then strangled 'in a macabre re-enactment of the video footage'. This real-life story also has implications for interpreting the effects of the media on anti-social behaviour (see Chapter 10).

Experimental support

In studies that support his theory, Zillmann and Bryant (1974) had participants pedal cycles to create either a high- or low-physiological arousal condition and following this had them play in a game where a confederate verbally abused them. Later they had the opportunity to deliver a harsh noise in the abuser's headphones. Zillmann's theory was supported because those in the high-arousal condition gave the higher level of noise intensity to the abuser.

In a later study, Bryant and Zillmann (1979) found that even one week later those in the high-arousal condition demonstrated more aggressiveness. However, after such a time lapse physiological arousal could no longer be present so other factors had to be responsible.

Zillmann (1988) consequently revised his initial theory to include a reappraisal of the situation. In fact he suggested that three factors interact:

1 physiological arousal;
2 learned dispositions or habits; and
3 interpretation of the arousal.

To demonstrate his suggestion empirically, Zillmann performed another study. Before being given the opportunity to retaliate, participants (in either a high- or low-arousal condition) were either given reasons why the abuser had behaved in such a way (e.g. he was suffering from stress) or they were given no explanation. Results showed that from the low-arousal condition the 'no explanation' group behaved aggressively toward the abuser, but where mitigating information was provided the low-arousal group reappraised the situation and directed less aggression at the abuser. In other words, if the recipient perceives the cause of the behaviour to be unintentional or there to be mitigating circumstances then an aggressive response is much less likely than if the attack is perceived to be either intentional or deliberate.

Evaluation

In the study by Zillmann above, the results for the low-arousal group are explained by the theory. But what about the high-arousal group? It was found that participants in this group, even though they heard the mitigating circumstances, behaved just as aggressively as those in the no-explanation group. Why did this happen? The answer may be that when we are mildly or even moderately aroused we retain the ability to process complex information about others and make an attribution that may well prevent us from behaving in a way that we may regret. However, when we are highly aroused we 'see red' and our arousal reduces any attributions we may make, or inhibitions we may have, and so we act in a way that we will regret.

Progress exercise

Is the excitation theory true to real life? What do you think: do you respond aggressively up to a week after you have been aroused in some way? Or, can you control your 'potentially aggressive urges' as suggested in the next section.

Cognitive neo-associationism

In an apparent attempt to incorporate the growing body of evidence suggesting that there is more to aggression than retaliation to aversive stimuli, Berkowitz (1989) outlined the **cognitive neo-associationist** view (Figure 7.1). Berkowitz suggests that exposure to aversive events generates **negative affect** (or unpleasant feelings). These feelings have to be reduced in some way and two options are at the individual's

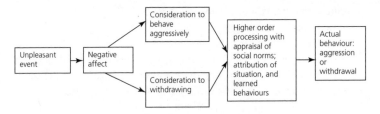

Figure 7.1 **The cognitive neo-associationist view of aggression**

disposal: either to behave aggressively or to escape from the situation by withdrawing. This is nothing new. What Berkowitz has added, however, is that the option a person chooses depends on how the person appraises the situation, taking into account the prevailing social norms and the type of attribution applied to the cause of the aversive stimuli. Another feature of this is whether or not the individual has learned to be aggressive as a means of coping with unpleasant situations.

There is a great deal of evidence to support the view that cognitive processing and attributions are important factors in determining our actual behaviour. It will seen in Chapter 8 that the consumption of alcohol leads to a person being more likely to take into account social or situational cues (such as provocation by others; encouragement by others to aggress) which suggest to the person what form of behaviour is appropriate in the circumstances. In effect, we now need to consider the extent to which the context in which an event occurs affects behaviour.

The social construction of aggression

A number of social psychologists argue that aggression is not an isolated individual act but one that can only be understood with reference to the social context in which it occurs.

According to Hewstone (1988) aggression is a social construction because of the factors that lead us to define an aggressive act as either anti- or pro-social. Such factors are determined by the social group with which we identify, and so contrasting interpretations may be provided by different groups for the same event. For example, in the Zimbardo (1969) deindividuation study (see p. 94) it is argued that dividing participants into groups led them to behave according to the presumed norms of their group.

If anti-social behaviour can be understood only with reference to the social context in which it occurs, then not only will there be differences within a society, and even regions and groups of the same society, but there will also be differences between societies.

Impression management

Another facet of the social construction of aggression is taken by Felson (1978), who sees it simply as a means of impression management. He argues that most of us create favourable identities for ourselves by, for example, being polite and co-operative. In some situations (such as in a prison) aggression is used as a way of maintaining the reputation of someone who must be treated with respect (or else!). In this way aggression can be understood only with reference to the situation in which it occurs.

Social constructionism and aggressive crowds

The view that when in groups we act according to the social identity of the group has been taken a step further by Reicher (1984b), who cites violent incidents involving **aggressive crowds**. His classic example is the 'riot' that happened in the St Paul's district of Bristol in 1980.

One afternoon the police raided a café following allegations of illegal drinking. Two men were arrested but as the police tried to leave, bricks were thrown at them. The violence escalated and police reinforcements were also attacked by a 'mob' of some three thousand who overturned cars and set them alight. One interpretation of this could be that each member of the group had lost his or her distinctiveness and uniqueness, could not be identified, and had become 'deindividuated' and, thus, more likely to perform anti-social acts. This suggests though, that such violent behaviour is likely to be 'mindless'. Reicher believes this explanation to be incorrect. He suggests instead that the crowd, the residents of the St Paul's area, had a common social identity as members of that community and saw the police as an illegitimate foreign presence which had to be removed. The incidents of violence were not mindless but were quite specific, selective and restrained:

- the violence was restricted to the specific St Paul's district;
- only police cars were damaged (and those suspected of being unmarked police cars);
- there was minimal damage to buildings;
- other outbreaks of violence were quickly stopped.

Another relevant example where the perceptions of anti-social behaviour differ according to the social group to which one belongs is football 'hooliganism'. The media frequently report on violent acts performed by football hooligans and preventive measures taken by police to combat such aggression. For many outside observers their 'social construction' leads them to believe that any action taken by the police is to be condoned. Alternatively, football supporters who engage in 'supporter rituals' perceive the police to be discriminating, harsh and even brutal against them. Rather than being a 'mindless mob of hooligans', according to Marsh et al. (1978), football fans operate within a strong social structure and their behaviour is highly patterned and ritualised. Despite threat displays such as taunts and gestures, very little violence actually happens. This may be true, but incidents of hooliganism and violence, reported both before and after football matches, suggest that the violence is real.

Deindividuation and anti-social behaviour

In the section on pro-social behaviour a whole chapter was devoted to the important affect of bystanders on behaviour (Chapter 5). For anti-social behaviour the effect other people may have is also important. Stated simply, it has been found that individuals are more likely to perform anti-social acts when they cannot be identified.

Whereas individuation is the differentiation of individuals from one another, deindividuation is a lack of distinctiveness and uniqueness. Initially the term deindividuation was used to explain why participating in crowd behaviour can diminish awareness of individuality. The theory is that in a large crowd each person is nameless and personal responsibility is diffused as each is faceless and anonymous. There is diminished fear of retribution and a diluted sense of guilt. The larger the group the greater the anonymity and the more difficult the identification of a single individual. Later Zimbardo (1969) distinguished between individuated behaviour, which is rational, consistent and conforms to all indicators of acceptable behaviour by society, and deindividuated behaviour, which is based on primitive urges, such as delinquent acts of violence and theft, which do not conform to society's norms of acceptability.

Laboratory studies of deindividuation

In a study performed by Zimbardo in 1969 female participants arrived at a laboratory. Half of the participants were greeted by name and wore name badges to enhance their individuality. In a second group the participants wore laboratory coats and hoods that masked their faces and they were much less identifiable than those in the first group. Even the experimenters did not know their names. The participants then heard a tape recording of an interview in which the 'victim' was portrayed either as altruistic and likeable or as self-centred and obnoxious. Participants then discovered that the study involved empathy judgements and the 'victim' was to be conditioned using electric shocks. The dependent variable was the length of time a single shock was given to the victim. Zimbardo found that those who were deindividuated delivered the shocks for nearly twice as long as those who were identifiable. Interestingly, whereas those in the individuated group gave a much longer shock to the obnoxious, self-centred victim compared to the likeable one, those who were deindividuated gave equivalent shocks to each.

In a very similar laboratory study, Prentice-Dunn and Rogers (1983) compared two groups of participants who were either individuated or deindividuated. In the individuated group participants wore name tags, were addressed by their first names, and the experimenter took an interest in the shock intensity given. Participants were also told that they would meet the victim afterwards and that the victim's well-being was their responsibility. The study was performed in a well-lit room. In the deindividuated condition names were not used, and the experimenter did not have any interest in the intensity of the shock given. Participants were told that they would not meet the victim afterwards and that the experimenter would take full responsibility for the well-being of the victim. The study was performed in a dimly lit room. Prentice-Dunn and Rogers found that the deindividuated group gave many more shocks than the other group but they also found the deindividuated participants did not feel inhibited, and showed no concern for the feelings of the victim, or the other members of the groups and not even the experimenter!

Deindividuation in children

Not only is it adults who behave in anti-social ways when they are deindividuated but children also behave in such a way. Hallowe'en is the 31st of October (my birthday!) and children typically engage in 'trick-or-treat' which involves dressing up in costumes and masks and calling at houses to presumably be tricked or treated! The masks and costumes give children anonymity and this gave Diener et al. (1976) the opportunity for a study. Diener et al. arranged for some children to call at homes by themselves and for others to call in groups. The person at each house was an accomplice of the experimenter who sometimes asked for their names and addresses and sometimes did not. This presented a triple opportunity for deindividuation: wearing a mask, being in a group, and not giving name or address. Would such children be more likely to behave anti-socially than those who were not deindividuated? As the children entered each house the accomplice pointed to a table, told each trick or treater to take one piece of candy, and then left the room. A hidden observer who was watching the children noted whether they helped themselves to the one piece of candy as instructed or whether they took more than one, or whether they took money which was in a bowl on the table. The results are shown in Table 7.2 and, as can be seen, the children who were in a

Table 7.2 **Deindividuation versus individuation in trick-or-treaters**

	Percentage of children who stole in each condition	
	Child alone	Child in group
Known to adult	7.5%	20.8%
Anonymous to adult	21.4%	57.2%

group and who were anonymous stole far more than children in any other group.

Developing the deindividuation hypothesis, Zimbardo and Fraser believed that anonymity would be greater in a large city than in a small town. To test this hypothesis they carried out a field study where they left a second-hand car on a street. When the car was left near the Bronx Campus of New York University the car was stripped of all removable items within twenty-six hours. In Palo Alto, a small town, a similar car was left at the same time. Twenty-six hours later the car in the small town remained intact.

Extremes of deindividuation

It can be concluded from the evidence presented above that people will behave much more anti-socially when they cannot see their victim or when their victim cannot see them. In the United States members of the terrorist Ku Klux Klan wear hoods not only to hide their identity from the police but also to submerge their identity into the group.

Deindividuation is also the basis on which much of modern warfare takes place. It can be argued that warfare today is carried out by people who are deindividuated. Those launching bombs and missiles using modern technology simply press buttons. They never see the enemy and the enemy never sees them. The famous 'electric shock' studies by Milgram (1963) demonstrate precisely this effect. The original impetus for Milgram's research was the extreme obedience to Nazi authority displayed by many German military personnel during World War II. Milgram's goal was to determine whether people of different nationalities differ in the extent to which they would obey authority. In the original study Milgram found a significant number, some 65 per cent of American male participants, continued to obey authority to the maximum of 450 volts. It is the series of follow-up studies, some eighteen in all, which are important here. For example, in 1965 Milgram found that people were more willing to administer shocks when the participants could not see the victim and when the victim could not see them. Milgram also found that by putting the teacher and learner in the same room, in close proximity, obedience was significantly reduced. Similarly, when face-to-face with the learner and required to force the learner's hand down on to a shock plate, only 30 per cent of teachers obeyed. It is for this reason that hoods were often placed over the heads of execution victims and in World War II the Nazi killings of Jews were carried out in gas chambers; well out of sight of the persons pressing the button.

There is yet more evidence of the impact deindividuation has on warfare. Watson (1973) generalised from the use of hoods to create anonymity and hypothesised that it is not only the use of hoods but of any form of disguise to change physical appearance when going into battle. He examined war records from twenty-three different countries and found those societies which used disguises, such as face and or body paint, were much more likely to engage in extreme aggression such as torture and execution.

In his famous social commentary, *Lord of the Flies*, William Golding used this idea to portray the way civilisation crumbled into anarchy when the boys painted their faces and became a savage tribe.

Evaluation

It is worth noting that in the Zimbardo laboratory study all the participants were women, and not men as was traditional in United States psychology studies. However, the tradition of using students was maintained, particularly those from introductory psychology classes.

In the Zimbardo field study there were so many variables that were uncontrolled that it is impossible to conclude that the size of town determined the damage to the vehicle.

Often deindividuation and anonymity are treated synonymously but it is possible to be anonymous without becoming deindividuated. For example, other forms of collective experience and shared awareness do not involve collective aggression, as shown in studies of peaceful crowds. Reicher (1984a) argues that, rather than automatically thinking in terms of deindividuation to explain the behaviours referred to in this section, we should look at the social identity developed by those allocated to a particular group as a plausible alternative.

Summary

This chapter has considered both social and cognitive explanations of anti-social behaviour. The original frustration-aggression hypothesis led to many studies being performed, mainly in the laboratory. The frustration-aggression hypothesis had a number of weaknesses and was modified. It also stimulated further research, particularly into what became known as the 'weapons effect' which has been found in a variety of cultures. Zillmann's excitation transfer theory links arousal and cognition and, from the research findings, Zillmann revised his initial idea. How situations and the causes of a behaviour are perceived is important. Theories emphasising such cognitive processing have led to the social cognitive theory and the cognitive neo-associationist view being proposed. Social constructionists argue that all behaviour, whether anti-social or not, needs to be understood in terms of the context in which it takes place. Deindividuational explanations emphasise a lack of distinctiveness and uniqueness, believing individuals are more likely to behave anti-socially when they are part of a group and they cannot be identified.

Review exercise

Essay question: Outline social psychological explanations of anti-social behaviour. Discuss social psychological explanations of anti-social behaviour.

Further reading

Berkowitz, L. (1998) *Aggression: Its Causes, Consequences and Control*. McGraw-Hill. Up-to-date views from a major author in this field.

Felson, R.B. & Tedeschi, J.T. (1993) Aggression and violence: social interactionist perspectives. *American Psychological Association*. The emphasis of this text is in its title.

8

Individual and environmental explanations of anti-social behaviour

 Anti-social behaviour and the individual
Anti-social behaviour and environmental psychology
Summary

Anti-social behaviour and the individual

Personality and aggression

Another set of factors which may explain anti-social behaviour are those related to personality. **Type A behaviour**, a label first coined by Friedman and Rosenman (1974), is exhibited by a person who is highly motivated, competitive, assertive, time-conscious and . . . aggressive. A number of studies have shown that type As are more likely to engage in hostile aggression. Type As are more likely than type Bs to:

- experience conflict at work;
- engage in child or spouse abuse (Strube et al. 1984);
- suffer extreme frustration when, for example, they are held up in traffic;
- demonstrate their 'road rage' by behaving aggressively not via rude gestures, but in terms of actual bodily harm to those perceived to have caused the problem;
- have road accidents: this was found by Evans et al. (1987) when

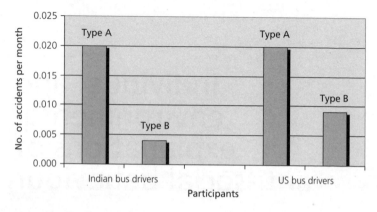

Figure 8.1 **Type A drivers have more accidents than type B drivers**

Source: Evans et al. 1987

studying bus drivers in both India and the United States. Type A drivers had accidents more frequently than type B drivers did, irrespective of country.

Dispositional anti-social behaviour

Acts of aggression are sometimes committed by people who become extremely frustrated. But why is it that some people continually behave aggressively? Surely the situations in which they find themselves cannot lead to so many frustrating incidents. Is aggression dispositional rather than situational?

If aggression is dispositional then it needs to be shown to be consistent. A number of specific studies have been done on the stability of aggression and each arrives at the same conclusion: that aggression in children becomes aggression in adults. Olweus (1979) has shown that highly aggressive 3-year-olds are likely to become aggressive 5-year-olds and that the physical and verbal aggression displayed at ages 6 to 10 is a good predictor of his or her tendency to continue at the same level at ages 10 and 14. Olweus has also found correlations of 0.79, some with data over twenty-one years apart, which clearly demonstrates the stability in aggression as dispositional rather than situational.

Studies by Huesmann et al. (1988) found significant correlations between peer assessments of aggression at 8 years of age and self- and spouse-reported aggression and criminal records over twenty-two years later. Farrington (1989) found that 22.4 per cent of those rated as highly aggressive by teachers at age 12 later had a conviction for violence.

Determinants of dispositional aggression

If aggression is dispositional, is it inherited? The simple answer to this question is that it is not. The more likely answer is that it is due to family environment where violent behaviours are modelled, rehearsed and reinforced. In fact, it is widely accepted that cold and rejecting parents who apply physical punishment in an erratic fashion, and often permit their child to express aggressive impulses, are to blame for their child's subsequent aggression. Indeed, parents who are inconsistent in carrying out threats and who fail to praise any socially desirable behaviour are likely to have children who present behaviour problems.

Patterson (1980) focuses on another aspect and distinguishes between coercive and non-coercive home environments. In a coercive environment, family members fight coercion with counter-coercion. This means that if two children have an argument one will learn to scream or shout to get the other to stop. If the children continue, a parent may intervene and use punitive and coercive tactics. However, the children then scream or shout at the mother to get her to stop and for peace the mother does so. However, in doing this she has lost the battle and even the war, because the children will use their counter-coercion strategy in future. By contrast, non-coercive parents do not cave-in but stand firm, ensuring their threat is carried through.

Shaffer (1985) takes this idea a step further and suggests that it is not just the family which is responsible for accounting for the stability of aggression but the child's peers too. A cyclical model is proposed to explain the process.

Evaluation

Despite family theories appearing to explain the stability of aggression, they are not as widely accepted as the theories emphasising delinquent

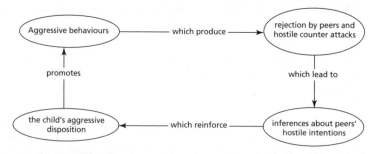

Figure 8.2 Cyclical model of peer influence on aggression

Source: adapted from Shaffer 1985: 497

friendships. Things have moved on a touch further because Elliot et al. (1985) propose an integrated theory which suggests that violent offending is the outcome of deficient family bonding, the learning of aggression in families, and strong bonding with deviant peers. Caspi et al. (1989) go a stage further and suggest that **cumulative continuity,** as they call it, is when a person selects environments that sustain the disposition. An aggressive person will select aggressive friends who will frequent hostile environments, for example. To short-circuit the trend, **interactional continuity** is needed.

Alcohol consumption and aggression

Does alcohol consumption lead to aggression? The commonly held view is that violence is increased by alcohol consumption, and that the more alcohol consumed, the worse the level of aggression. Taylor and Gammon (1976) gave participants either high levels of alcohol (apparently three or four stiff drinks) or low levels (one drink) and then were given the opportunity to deliver an electric shock. They found that the more alcohol consumed, the greater the level of aggression (as measured by number of electric shocks). In a review of studies on alcohol and aggression by Hull and Bond (1986) the overwhelming conclusion is that violence is increased by the consumption of alcohol. However, other studies have shown that the amount of alcohol is unrelated to the level of aggression. Why is this? What explanations have been proposed to explain the relationship between alcohol and aggression?

One suggestion is that alcohol affects the brain by releasing primitive urges to respond aggressively. If this were true it would mean that most if not all people would be unable to control aggressive outbursts when they consume alcohol. Clearly this just does not happen.

A second suggestion is that the alcohol reduces the constraints a person usually has in place preventing aggressive behaviour from happening, but interestingly, as shown by Steele and Southwick (1985), the removal of such inhibitions can also lead to an increase in helping behaviour.

A more likely explanation is provided by Taylor and Sears (1988) who propose that alcohol interferes with normal cognitive functioning. In their study male participants consumed what they thought was a large amount of alcohol. One group consumed alcohol but the other consumed liquid that smelled and looked alcoholic but was not. Participants then competed in a reaction time test against each other where an electric shock was given to the loser. An accomplice of the experimenter initially encouraged participants to give ever-increasing shocks, and left the room after a period of time. Results showed that the level of shocks remained consistent throughout for the non-alcoholic group, whilst the 'alcoholic group' initially gave larger shocks when encouraged by the accomplice but later reduced the level of shock when the accomplice left the room. It can be concluded from this that alcohol does not automatically cause an increase in aggression. Taylor and Sears believe that alcohol influences normal cognitive functioning to the extent that we are more likely to take into account social or situational cues (such as strong provocation; encouragement to aggress by others) which suggest what form of behaviour is appropriate for the person to choose in the circumstances. This could well be aggressive behaviour or it could lead the person to withdraw.

Sexual arousal and aggression

The link between sexual arousal and aggression was thoroughly investigated in the United States in the early 1970s and in one study, after exposing male participants to pornographic photographs, films and books for one-and-a-half hours for fifteen consecutive days, the conclusion drawn was that 'pornography is an innocuous stimulus which leads quickly to satiation and that public concern over it is misplaced'. Howard et al. (1973: 133). However, there is a little more to it than this: pornography still frequently portrays violence against women, and many studies have shown that there is a link between sexual arousal and aggression.

The above contradiction is also evident in laboratory studies. In a study by Baron (1974) male participants were angered by an accomplice of the experimenter and then exposed either to photographs of 'highly attractive nude women taken from *Playboy* magazine' or to photographs of scenery or abstract art. They were then given the opportunity to aggress against the accomplice. Baron found that those shown the scenery and abstract art gave *higher* levels of shock than those shown sexually arousing photographs. On the other hand Jaffe et al. (1974) carried out a very similar study except that they showed participants highly explicit erotic passages, rather than *Playboy* photographs. Jaffe et al. found the opposite to Baron: that erotic material led to higher levels of shock than neutral materials.

How can this apparent contradiction be explained? Zillman's two-factor theory provides an explanation. Exposure to erotic material causes arousal and when we are mildly or even moderately aroused we can still process information about others and make an appropriate attribution (as may have been the case in the Baron study). However, when we are highly aroused (as in the Jaffe et al. study) this reduces any ability to make attributions in a logical way and so we may behave in a way that may be more extreme than usual. Crucially, there may well be a world of difference between participants knowing they are taking part in a laboratory study and people behaving intimately in private.

Progress exercise

Discussion points. Provide two arguments for and two arguments against: Alcohol consumption leads to aggression; sexual arousal and aggression are correlated in men but not women.

Gender differences in aggression: biological or social?

The conclusion that can be drawn from over a hundred studies is that not only are girls less likely than boys to remain aggressive, they are less aggressive in the first place!

The biological view claims that sex differences in aggression are due to androgens (sex hormones), particularly levels of testosterone in males. Gladue (1991) took samples of blood from both male and female participants and analysed them for hormone levels, particularly testosterone. Results showed that higher concentrations of testosterone were associated with higher levels of self-reported aggression (physical, verbal and impulsive) in males, whereas in females, high concentrations of testosterone were associated with lower levels of aggression.

Konner (1982) found that among male prison inmates the higher the levels of testosterone, the earlier the age of first arrest.

Some social psychologists would argue that males and females are provided with different socialisation experiences, which leads them to perceive aggression differently. For example, boys are taught that aggression is appropriate by parents perhaps telling a crying boy to 'go and hit the child back'. For girls the opposite is the case, parents stressing that aggression is 'unfeminine' and 'just for boys'.

Anti-social behaviour and environmental psychology

You may recall that in Chapter 4 we said that environmental psychology was concerned with the way in which we interact with the environment: that it influences us and we modify it in most things we do. Of course, environmental psychology does not just look at how various factors influence pro-social behaviour, it also looks at how environmental factors affect anti-social behaviour. For example, temperature, noise and crowding were seen to affect helping behaviour. Those very same factors will now be looked at to see to what extent they affect our anti-social behaviours.

Temperature

Ambient temperature describes the surrounding or atmospheric conditions. However, the perception of temperature is psychological and we become too hot or too cold when we reach the extremes of our bodily core temperature. There is no doubt, according to Anderson (1989), that heat *causes* aggression. Specifically, as the temperature moves from comfortable to hot, crimes against people, such as assaults, or domestic violence, and sex crimes, such as rape, increase. Anderson's evidence is based on a two-year study carried out in Houston, Texas. He found that the higher the daily temperature, the greater the incidence of violent crime.

In the Unites States in the 1960s there were many riots and a popular belief was that they were *caused* by heat discomfort. The US Riot Commission published data stating that of all the riots in 1967 all but one occurred on days when the temperature was above 27°C (or 80°F). Many commentators began to refer to it as 'the long hot summer effect'. Baron and Ransberger (1978) similarly found that the number of riots in the United States between 1967 and 1971 increased as the temperature rose. Baron and Bell (1977) conclude that there is a critical range of uncomfortably warm ambient temperatures (between 81° and 85° Fahrenheit) which facilitates aggressive responses in humans but that extremely high or cold temperatures reduce aggression.

Evaluation

So is it correct that high temperature causes riots and/or aggression? The simple answer is that it is not correct. Just because a number of high correlations are found, cause and effect cannot be assumed. In most cases it is not the heat that causes anti-social behaviour but some other trigger which the heat makes worse. For example, it is argued that the cause of the US riots was the unrest related to the civil liberties movements. It just happened to be good weather at the same time, which led people to make incorrect assumptions.

Whilst studies show that the number of riots increases with higher temperatures, they also show that there are fewer riots and crimes against people when it grows too hot: this is simply because it is too hot to do anything, let alone have a riot! Why does anti-social behaviour increase and decrease in this way? There is evidence that heat and aggression are related, but why is this? A number of theories may provide the answer.

Theories of temperature and aggression

The Baron and Bell (1977) negative affect escape model predicts that up to a point heat will increase aggression but as the heat becomes extremely uncomfortable aggression decreases. Low temperature has little effect but as the temperature increases the discomfort experienced also increases and aggression is more likely. However, if the temperature becomes too high then it is too hot to behave aggressively and so the level of aggression decreases.

The Zillmann two-factor theory (see Chapter 7, p. 88ff) proposes that an increase in temperature causes an increase in arousal. If we explain the arousal as being caused by the heat we will not behave aggressively. However, if we do not attribute the increased arousal to the heat but to some person who has caused us annoyance then we are more likely to behave aggressively toward that person.

Density and crowding

As mentioned in Chapter 4 crowding is a psychological concept created by either spatial (e.g. size of room) or social (number of people) density. In the laboratory aggressiveness appears to be related to spatial rather than social density. Many studies have been performed on crowding in the laboratory and various effects have been discovered. For example, it has been found that in conditions of limited space men are generally more aggressive than females but the effect is very small and the levels of aggressiveness very mild. Studies have been performed on children and seemingly have produced inconsistent results. Aiello et al. (1979), for example, found that increased density led to more aggression in children but this finding has been contradicted by other studies, one of which found no effect, while another found that decreased density led to more aggression! The crucial point here is related to how aggression is measured. In the studies on children the experimenters observed how aggressively children played with the toys they provided for them. They thus increased the spatial density and observed the behaviour of the children. Naively, they did not control for the number of toys provided and the levels of aggression related not to the spatial density but to the frustration the children experienced by having too few toys per child to play with.

Aggression and density are more easily measurable in real-life settings such as crowding in prisons. Here increases in disciplinary infringements have been correlated with increased population density, as have aggressive behaviours. Cox et al. (1984) found that in one prison a 30 per cent decrease in numbers resulted in a 60 per cent decrease in assaults. When a 20 per cent increase in numbers occurred there was a 36 per cent increase in assaults.

Noise

Sound is created by rapidly changing air pressure at the eardrum. Some sounds can be pleasant but unwanted sound is simply noise. Noise is, therefore, psychological. Your favourite piece of music could be noise to someone else. Psychologists have studied the effect of noise on aggression in a number of ways. In laboratory studies, Geen and O'Neil (1969) found that people who had seen a film featuring aggression and were subsequently exposed to noise, consisting of a two-minute burst of white noise at 60dB, gave more electric shocks (average of 4.58) when compared to participants who were not exposed to noise (3.16 shocks average). Of course, although no shocks are actually given, this is unethical.

In 1976 Donnerstein and Wilson found that unpredictable and uncontrollable bursts of noise increased the aggression of angry participants – as measured by intensity of electric shock. In their study as participants worked on unsolvable mathematical problems to make them angry they were exposed either to no noise, 95dB of unpredictable and uncontrollable noise, or to 95dB of unpredictable noise that they believed they could turn off at any time. Finally, participants were then either made angry or not by the experimenter accomplice who would then be the recipient of the electric shocks. A number of conclusions can be drawn from the results (see Figure 8.3):

1 shock intensity is higher when participants are angry;
2 shock intensity is lower when the noise is controllable.

In real life, excessive noise caused by neighbours which other residents have been unable to control has led to a number of incidents of aggression against the noisemakers. In one extreme example, Peter Thurston was jailed for twenty-two years for firebombing his noisy

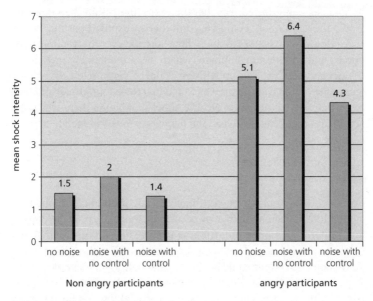

Figure 8.3 **Uncontrollable and unpredictable noise makes angry participants behave more aggressively**

neighbours. Apparently, 'he was so driven by the relentless noise of parties within that block which spanned over a decade, that he planned and executed this terrible attack' (*Daily Mirror*, 1995: 9). In another incident, Allan Moynihan had frequently complained to police about the noise outside his home and as nothing was done he lined up teenager Lee Hickman in his air-rifle sights and shot him, severing an artery in his neck (*Daily Mail*, Wednesday 23 February 2000: 41).

Unpleasant odours

Yet another environmental factor that has been found to affect aggression is unpleasant odours. Whilst there are many odours emanating from various industrial processes, the evidence on how these affect aggression is difficult to evaluate. In a laboratory situation it is rather different as both the odours and the response to them can be carefully controlled. Rotton et al. (1979) discovered in their laboratory study that unpleasant odours affect aggression. The hypothesis being tested was that the more unpleasant the odour the worse the aggression would be. Rotton et al. exposed participants to two odours: ethyl mercaptan (which has an extremely unpleasant odour) and ammonium sulphide (which has a moderately unpleasant odour) and a control group with no odour. Using the electric shock technique outlined earlier, it was found that the odour groups did lead to participants giving more electric shocks, although there was not a significant difference between the responses to the moderate and the extreme odours.

Summary

For any behaviour to be attributed to an individual it must be shown to occur on a number of occasions, that is, it must be consistent rather than a once-in-a-lifetime event. Dispositional anti-social behaviour could arise from a variety of sources, such as the family. Anti-social behaviour could be due to personality, for example a Type A personality is more likely to engage in road rage than a Type B personality. The tendency to behave anti-socially could be enhanced through the consumption of alcohol or the viewing of pornographic material.

Anti-social behaviour has been shown to be more likely to occur if the outdoor temperature is hot (but not too hot); if people are crowded; if they are exposed to uncontrollable, unpredictable and loud noise or if they are exposed to extremely unpleasant odours.

Review exercise

1. Give three pieces of experimental evidence suggesting that the environment may affect aggressive behaviour.
2. To what extent is dispositional aggression learned?

Further reading

Gifford, R. (1997, 2nd edn) *Environmental Psychology*. Allyn & Bacon. Excellent environment text including factors related to both anti-social and pro-social behaviour.

Hewstone, M. and Stroebe, W. (2001) *Introduction to Social Psychology* (3rd edn). Blackwell Publishers. Far more than an introduction here and up-to date.

9

Reducing and controlling anti-social behaviour

Controlling aggression with punishment
Catharsis and aggression reduction
Alternative strategies for aggression reduction
Summary

Fundamental to maintaining peace and order in any society is the control of anti-social behaviour. Generally, this can be done on two levels:

1 at a societal level through sanctions imposed by legitimate authority; or
2 at an individual level through the learning of appropriate behaviours or through controlling how we think about things.

Each of these will be considered in detail.

Controlling aggression with punishment

To the 'average person in the street' the most obvious way of reducing aggression is to punish it. If a child behaves aggressively we can remove privileges, discuss the issue and make the child realise the error and, for some people, the child is smacked. For an adult, a wrongdoing, depending on its nature, can be fined, given a prison sentence and, in some cultures, even executed. These behaviours are based on the behavioural assumption that the punishment will teach the transgressor a lesson and that in future the behaviour will not be repeated and so the punishment will be avoided: unless of course the punishment is death! But even this serves to act as a deterrent to others. Indeed, the concept behind the ancient custom of executions and punishments such as flogging and the use of stocks is that punishing a person for aggressive acts in public will deter others from committing those acts.

Punishment and children

There are two main options available:

1 Use of severe (physical) punishment. This type of punishment may well be effective in the short term but in the long term it can have the opposite effect. As was seen in Chapter 9, Sears et al (1957) amongst others have found that parents who use severe punishment tend to produce children who are aggressive themselves. However, it is difficult to draw firm conclusions from this because parents who use severe punishment probably do many other things in addition, such as being harsh and aggressive; they may even have an authoritarian personality and the child is simply copying their behaviour. Eron (1982) describes the case of Ronald, a very aggressive child. After observing Ronald, Eron concluded that 'the punitive atmosphere at home (in which Ronald's father frequently spanked him and washed his mouth out with soap) probably instigated Ronald to be aggressive both there and at school' (207).

2 Use of mild punishment. Whilst severe punishment may bring temporary compliance, what is needed is for the child to understand the error of his or her behaviour and behave appropriately for the right reasons. The use of mild threats has been found to be much more effective than threats of severe punishment. However, it is essential that the parent knows the child well in terms of what will and what will not work; that the parent is not prepared to back down; that there is a system of rewards in place for appropriate behaviours. In laboratory studies by Bandura (1965) and others the conclusion is that even if children observe models being punished

for behaving aggressively, children still behave more aggressively than those who have not seen aggression in the first place.

Punishment and adults

To address whether punishment imposed by legitimate authority is effective, we need to consider whether the threat of arrest and possible imprisonment acts as a deterrent for the majority of the population. For a large proportion of the population, the prospect of punishment is an additional, rather than the single most important, reason for not behaving aggressively toward others. For some people such punishment is not a deterrent, as reflected by the slow upward trend in crime statistics.

Bower and Hilgard (1981) suggest that punishment can be a successful deterrent if:

1 the punishment is *prompt*, and follows the aggressive act as soon as possible;
2 it is *intense* and highly aversive; and
3 it is *probable,* that is, it is almost always applied.

Evaluation

If this is the case why does punishment not seem to be working? One possibility is the delay between the event and the trial (and therefore punishment) and another possibility is that punishment is applied inconsistently. In the British legal system there have been many cases recently where drivers are given light sentences or even fines where they have killed another person because of their driving error and yet relatively minor offences receive prison sentences. It is also the case that countries which have the death penalty do not have fewer murders than countries who have abolished the death penalty.

Does punishment by imprisonment 'cure' the illegal aggressor? Some people do leave prison as 'reformed characters', but others do not (and even learn new anti-social behaviours in prison), probably because the conditions for effective punishment as outlined by Bower and Hilgard are not met.

Should Britain have abolished the death penalty?
Should countries such as the United States of America abolish their death penalty?

Catharsis and aggression reduction

How can aggressive energy be discharged? Dollard et al. (1939) believed that 'the expression of any act of aggression is a catharsis that reduces the instigation of all other acts of aggression'. 'Letting off steam' and 'getting it out of your system' are typical expressions describing catharsis. Freud (1933) believed that aggression should be directed into socially acceptable activities through sublimation or displacement, for example sports competitions. Thus, catharsis can work in two ways: either through engaging in direct aggression or through engaging in a form of physical activity such as sport.

Catharsis and direct aggression

Does engaging in direct aggression reduce the need for further aggression? In a laboratory study Geen (1978) paired each participant with an accomplice of the experimenter. During a discussion the accomplice gave the participant an electric shock (yes, an actual shock) when the participant disagreed. In the second part of the study the roles were reversed and some participants were given the opportunity to shock the accomplice whilst others merely recorded errors. Following this all participants were allowed to give shocks. If the previous shocking of the accomplice was cathartic there would be no need to shock the accomplice again. This was not found and participants who had given shocks previously gave even more shocks a second time around. Direct aggression, as found in this study, is not cathartic.

Another possibility is that children can be taught to be aggressive to inanimate objects such as Bobo dolls. However, Bandura in his early studies discovered that children who had aggressed against a Bobo doll were more rather than less aggressive in interactions with peers compared to children who had not bashed Bobo.

Catharsis and sport

Does engaging in a form of physical activity such as sport reduce the need for further aggression? It is worth extending this question and in addition asking 'Does observing aggressive sport act as a catharsis?'

In relation to the first question, there is the clear conclusion that engaging in vigorous activity does not act as a catharsis. Zillmann et al. (1972) compared the aggression levels of two groups: group one were provoked and then rode a bicycle and the other group were provoked but did no physical activity. If physical activity is cathartic then the first group should use the activity as an outlet and behave less aggressively than the group who had no outlet. Results showed exactly the opposite in that those exercising behaved more aggressively.

What about watching sport? Berkowitz takes the extreme view when he writes 'a decade of laboratory research has virtually demolished the contention that people will lessen their aggressive tendencies by watching other persons beat each other up' (1970: 2). In fact, not only has it been found that watching sport does not reduce aggression, it has been found that watching sport either has no effect on aggression or it actually increases it! Goldstein and Arms (1971) found spectators watching an American football match experienced increased feelings of hostility whereas gymnastics spectators did not. Arms et al. (1980) found that those watching contact sports (ice hockey and wrestling) reported more aggression than those watching non-contact competitive sports (swimming) did. These studies suggest therefore that, if anything, more rather than less aggression results from watching such activities.

A simple conclusion is sufficient: contrary to popular belief, catharsis is not an effective means of reducing aggression.

Alternative strategies for aggression reduction

Incompatible responses

The use of '**incompatible responses**' is based on the belief that it is difficult to do two incompatible things at once or have two incompatible emotions at the same time: so a person who is happy, for example, is much less likely to behave aggressively. In one demonstration of this Brown and Elliot (1965) asked teachers to ignore all aggressive acts but to reward all instances of pro-social behaviour. They found that within two weeks both physical and verbal aggression had reduced significantly.

Similarly teachers, parents and other significant role models can counteract aggressive tendencies by encouraging traits such as sensitivity, co-operation and empathy whilst at the same time discouraging inappropriate aggression and punishing negative behaviour in a non-physical way. If children can be taught empathy (see Midlarsky and Bryan 1967, ch. 2) then they are more likely to understand other people's feelings and become less hostile towards them. Bryant (1982) found that children who scored high on empathy scored low on aggression, whereas others who scored very low on empathy tended to be more aggressive.

Non-aggressive environments

Another possibility is to create non-aggressive environments. Based on what was said in earlier chapters, if children are provided with an environment where there are no aggressive toys (such as guns, knives and even 'Action Men') then there is nothing to suggest aggression to them. This would then counter 'the weapons effect' (see Chapter 7). Further, if children were provided with sufficient toys with which to play this would reduce aggression, as would teachers' providing equal access to them (see Barker et al. 1941 in Chapter 7, p. 80).

Attribution training

If individuals behave anti-socially because they misinterpret the cause of behaviour towards them, if they are able to consider alternative explanations, negative interpretations can be avoided.

Toch (1980) makes the observation that much of the violence in society appears to be present in those lacking in social skills. Toch claims that such individuals do not know how to express themselves, are insensitive to others, have an abrasive style of self-expression and so experience frustration because their inefficiency continually angers others. He thus suggests that social-skills training would either teach them to avoid potentially explosive situations or provide them with the necessary skills to ensure they can apply constructive criticism without creating anger or aggression in others.

Extending this strategy, studies have shown that providing a simple apology can be effective in reducing aggression. Ohbuchi et al. (1989) conducted a study which involved a participant and an experimenter's accomplice working on a problem-solving task. The accomplice deliberately made a mistake that ensured the task would fail. As a result the experimenter then criticised the participant for doing very poorly. The accomplice then either apologised to the participant or did not. Ohbuchi et al. found that participants were much less aggressive to the accomplice when they received the apology than when they received no apology for the accomplice's behaviour.

Counteracting deindividuation

Deindividuation, you may recall (see Chapter 7), is where individuals are more likely to perform anti-social acts when they cannot be identified. How can they be identified? Ainsworth and Pease (1987) suggest that individuals should be made aware that they can be singled out. This should then have the effect of making them think twice about what they do. One way of achieving this is to record who they are and what they are doing either by photograph or by videotape. At one recent football match involving violence, 'supporters' were 'named and shamed' in national newspapers. What should be even more successful is to show the faces of individuals on screens at football grounds which would enhance their self-awareness and reduce any deindividuation.

Summary

The control of anti-social behaviour can be done on two levels: individual and societal. The main way of controlling aggression is through punishment and this chapter looked at punishment in children as distinct from punishment in adults. For various reasons punishment is not considered to be a desirable strategy. An alternative is to consider the Freudian concept of catharsis and how sport could be used as an outlet. Other alternative strategies include: 'incompatible responses'; the provision of 'non-aggressive environments'; attribution training and ways in which deindividuation can be counteracted.

Review exercise

1. Give two reasons why punishment is said to be an effective deterrent. Give two why punishment is not always effective.
2. Describe what is meant by catharsis. Provide arguments for and against the view that sport is a successful outlet for aggression.

Section III

MEDIA INFLUENCES ON PRO- AND ANTI-SOCIAL BEHAVIOUR

10

Pro- and anti-social behaviour and the media

Pro-social behaviour and the media
Anti-social behaviour and the media
Studying the effects of television violence
Alternative media and aggression
The effects of watching television violence
Summary

We have seen that observational learning and reinforcement are important in learning aggressive or helping behaviour. What then, is the role of the media in this process; in particular what is the role of television? Television has been chosen as the main focus of attention for two reasons:

1 Television opens children's minds to vast worlds of experience that would otherwise be unavailable. Its potential for enhancing knowledge and experience is endless.
2 Television is now in more than 95 per cent of homes in Britain and is switched on for an average of 25–30 hours per week. In the United States children between 6 and 11 years watch twenty-five hours per week and children aged 2–5 years watch even more. Barwise and Ehrenberg (1988) say that television is 'the giant among media'.

Pro-social behaviour and the media

If children watch a large amount of television then a logical approach is to ensure they watch pro- rather than anti-social programmes. The findings of many studies make it clear that the mere exposure of children to pro-social models encourages pro-social acts and in particular they are more likely to be repeated if they are rewarded. Can the same be achieved through watching pro-social television programmes?

Pro-social television programmes

Stein and Friedrich (1972) exposed children for four weeks to television involving one of three types of programme: aggressive, neutral or pro-social. Those in the pro-social condition subsequently showed more helpfulness, co-operation and affection than those in the other conditions. Similarly, Sprafkin et al. (1975) used programmes about the dog 'Lassie'. In one condition Lassie saves her puppies by barking for help; in another Lassie is involved but does not exhibit pro-social behaviour. Later the children are playing a game where they can earn points. During the game they hear a puppy's barking which suggests it may need help. Would those from the pro-social Lassie condition show more helpful behaviour, and even forgo game points, than those in the neutral Lassie group? They did, helping for an average of forty-one seconds longer than those in the other group.

Other studies have also targeted popular television programmes. Baran (1979) found 8- to 10-year-olds who had watched an episode of *The Waltons,* where helping behaviour was prominent in the storyline, later exhibited more helping behaviours than those who had not watched this episode. Forge and Phemister (1987) have found that when children of nursery school age are exposed to pro-social programmes such as *Sesame Street* they are more likely to behave in altruistic ways than children who have not had experience of such programmes. In fact the United States government created the Children's Television Workshop in 1968 to produce television programmes that would stimulate interest and intellectual development. Its first production, *Sesame Street*, is now broadcast in nearly seventy countries worldwide.

Studies by Messenger-Davies (1989) reveal that watching television serves many useful purposes:

- it informs children, helping to structure their lives;
- it gives common interests with friends and family, providing family togetherness, discussion and argument;
- it gives children ideas for play and work; it is one form of entertainment.

Gunter and McAleer (1990) draw the same conclusions, claiming that television can have socially desirable effects through educational programmes, entertainment and drama productions. It is claimed that good informative programmes can introduce children to a wide range of people, places and ideas; that such programmes help children to keep in touch with their peers who watch the same programmes.

Anti-social to pro-social

Rather than focusing on pro-social programmes it is also possible to make what could be argued to be anti-social programmes more pro-social. Geller (1988) observed the use of seat belts by United States television personalities on prime-time television between 1984 and 1986. Geller found that both drivers and passengers rarely wore seat belts and considered that this was irresponsible on the part of television companies, given the image they were creating not only for children but for viewers of all ages. The subsequent nationwide campaign, which at one point had some 800 schoolchildren write to 'Mr T', a character from the *A-Team* programme, to complain, was successful in that there was a significant increase in seat belt usage by television personalities and Mr T increased from no belt use to 70 per cent belt use.

List three pro-social television programmes. What message do they carry? List three films you have seen that you think set bad examples. Why list *these* films?

Progress exercise

Anti-social behaviour and the media

Imitation follows observation

Whilst we desire children to observe and imitate pro-social images, we do not wish them to observe and imitate anti-social images. However, the powerful effect of anti-social images influences not only children but also the behaviour of adults. Consider the following examples:

- In 1973 a group of youths doused a woman in petrol and set fire to her, reproducing a scene from the film *Fuzz* shown two days earlier.
- The number of 'accidental' suicides increased significantly in the US after the showing of the film *Deerhunter* with the Russian roulette scene.
- In 1981 John Hinckley, Jr. attempted to assassinate President Regan. Hinckley was said to be a 'media freak' whose hero was Travis Bickle, a gun-slinging hero of the film *Taxi Driver*.
- In 1977 Ronald Zamora was accused of murdering an 83-year-old woman. His lawyers argued that he was 'not guilty by reason of insanity because of his intoxication with television'. He was found guilty.
- In Killeen, Texas a man drove his truck through the window of a cafeteria and then shot twenty-two people. In his pocket was a receipt for the film *Fisher King* in which a deranged man fired a shotgun into a crowded bar.
- Reported in the media in September 1995 in Britain was the case of the 6-year-old girl who shot dead her grandfather as she copied a scene from a Sylvester Stallone film (rated PG) she had just watched on video. The newspaper headline read, 'Six-year-old blasts a grandfather with his own revolver as she acts out a movie scene' and followed it with 'she copied a scene from a Sylvester Stallone film she had just watched on video'.

The crucial point about all the examples above, except the last, is that they all involve adults. It is not just children who imitate the violence they have seen, although it is children on whom most studies concentrate.

The first evidence that witnessed aggression could lead to imitation by observers of it was the work of Bandura in the 1960s (see Chapter

6 for details). Since then many studies have been carried out on the link between television violence and aggressive behaviour, using a variety of methods.

Studying the effects of television violence

Laboratory studies of the link between media and aggression

The short-term effects of television violence have been investigated in a number of ways. In controlled laboratory conditions a number of studies have shown that when children are exposed to more violent programmes they show more violent attitudes and behaviour.

Following the studies of Bandura (1965), where participants watched filmed violence in a laboratory, many other studies followed in which excerpts of filmed violence were shown rather than real-life instances using Bobo dolls and the like. One early study was done by Berkowitz and Geen (1966) who showed children either the aggressive film *Champion* or a non-aggressive film. It was found that those watching the aggressive film delivered more electric shocks than those watching the non-aggressive film (see Chapter 7 for details). These results support the view that aggression is triggered by a stimulus in the environment, and in this case the aggressive film was the catalyst.

Liebert and Baron (1972) showed children (boys and girls aged between 5 and 9 years of age) either violent and aggressive (fighting or shooting from the programme *The Untouchables*) or non-violent (tennis) excerpts from television. After this the children were shown two buttons on a panel. They were told that pushing one button would help another child win a prize, whilst pushing the other would hurt the child. The children were also told that the longer they pressed the button the more it would help or hurt the other child. As can be seen from Table 10.1, those watching the violence hurt the other child for significantly longer than those not watching the violence. This led Liebert and Baron to conclude that watching televised aggression can make children more willing to hurt another child.

More recently, Josephson (1987) conducted a study on 8- and 9-year-old-boys. These boys watched either an excerpt from a popular but violent television programme where the police killed a number of criminals or an excerpt about a motorcycle racing team. Later the boys played a game of 'floor hockey' that gave the experimenters

Table 10.1 Aggression following exposure to aggression

Television violence and aggression		non-violent excerpt	violent excerpt
Average duration of aggressive responses	boys	2.1	5.2
	girls	1.6	3.1

Source: adapted from Liebert and Baron 1972

an opportunity to observe their behaviour. The results were of no surprise: the boys who had been previously rated as aggressive by their teachers and who had seen the violent excerpt were much more likely to play the game aggressively. Those who had been rated as aggressive but who watched the non-violent excerpt were significantly less violent.

Evaluation

A number of criticisms have been aimed at studies that have been conducted in the laboratory. Whilst the laboratory does offer a number of advantages, such as control over extraneous variables, there are a number of other concerns:

- the laboratory is an artificial setting; often so are the measures which may involve an electric shock;
- a Bobo doll is not a real person; children know it is perfectly acceptable to bash Bobo;
- participants have been given permission to act aggressively and there is no fear of retaliation;
- the excerpts of films shown are quite brief and often consist of a single violent episode;
- brief segments of films do not allow the development of a plot; brief segments do not contain a mix of violent and non-violent interaction such as humour or romance;
- the laboratory situation is controlled and the participant is often isolated. At home the child will have other activities going on at the same time – the child can even consume milk and biscuits!

- learning aggressive acts in a laboratory does not mean the observer will perform those acts elsewhere;
- although laboratory studies demonstrate the immediate effects of television violence, they do not show lasting effects; for that the use of other methods such as naturalistic or longitudinal studies are needed.

Field studies of the media and aggression

The use of field studies would appear to overcome some of the problems encountered in laboratory studies. Leyens et al. (1975) studied boys in four dormitories at a boarding school for juvenile offenders. Measures of aggression were taken which was judged to be relatively high in two dormitories and relatively low in the other two. The boys then participated in 'Movie Week' where the experimenters manipulated what the boys watched. Two dormitories (one rated high- and one rated low-aggression) watched violent films and the other two dormitories (again, previously rated as high and low) watched non-violent films. The results of the study showed that for the high-aggression violent-film group 'the films evoked among the spectators the kind of aggression they had been exposed to' (353).

In the study by Parke et al. (1977) male juvenile delinquents who had been together for some time were used, and it was found that those who viewed the aggressive films were more physically and verbally violent towards the other children, but whether their behaviour was caused by watching the violence or whether they were predisposed towards violence by other factors is unknown. Of course, weight is added to the debate that the films were responsible because control groups were used – who, like the experimental groups, were also boy delinquents.

Longitudinal studies of the media and aggression

The aim of this type of research is to measure the child's violent viewing at a given time and then assess his or her aggressive behaviour at some later date. In a longitudinal study Lefkowitz et al. (1977) found a significant correlation between the amount of television watched by over 400 children of 8 and 9 years of age and their aggression at age 19 (ten years later). Notably, they conclude that it is not aggressive children who watch more television but that those who watch television violence are later judged to be aggressive.

Eron (1982) concluded from a longitudinal study that the relationship between television violence and subsequent aggression is a circular one. Television violence is one cause of aggression but aggressive children prefer to watch violent television. Thus, continued viewing causes further aggression and the cycle continues.

To try to establish some evidence of causality, Milavsky et al. (1982) performed a longitudinal study of some 3,200 children. They concluded that there is no firm evidence relating television violence and violent behaviour, let alone providing evidence of a relationship. On the other hand, as will be explored later, several longitudinal studies suggest there is a clear link between television violence and aggressive behaviour in children.

Cross-cultural studies

Williams (1986) found towns in isolated areas of both Australia and Canada that do not have television reception but which are similar to towns with television reception in all other respects. Several differences were found: in the towns with no television reception children scored higher on reading tests, were physically fitter and less likely to be obese.

Slightly more convincing are the results gathered by Hennigan et al. (1982) who looked at the changes in crime rates following the introduction of television to areas where it was previously unavailable. Interestingly, they found no change in violent crime, but this analysis focused on reported crimes and did not consider the possibility of change in unreported crimes.

Huesmann and Eron (1988) found, from their studies in different countries, that the greater the percentage of television programmes with violent content, the higher the rate of violent crime and murder (Figure 10.1).

They are quick to point out that just because the data suggest that increased television violence determines murder rates there are likely to be many other factors that contribute to the differences.

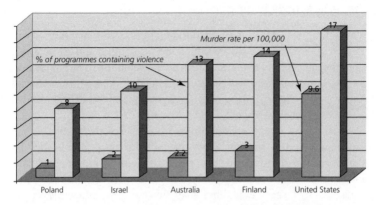

Figure 10.1 **The relationship between violent programmes and murder rates**

Alternative media and aggression

Video violence

Videotape is another medium through which violence can be watched. In many respects watching videotapes is worse than television because these can be watched at any time of day; they can be watched by children when parents are out; they can be watched many times; and frequently uncut versions are available. Newson is in no doubt that 'video nasties', as they have become known, are causing concern about what children watch. She says 'Over the past few years, considerable anxiety has been expressed by those professionally concerned with children about the effects of 'horror', 'sex and violence', 'soft porn' and similar scenes experienced by children via videos seen in their own or their friends' homes' (1994: 273).

Again, real-life examples of tragic events reinforce the concern expressed. The first example is the case of the two 10-year-old killers of James Bulger. Thompson and Venables regularly watched adult horror movies, including, it is claimed, the notorious *Child's Play 3*. Their murder of James Bulger in 1990 apparently involved acts they had watched. A second example involves a 15-year-old boy who carried out two armed robberies. His father blamed violent videos for his son's descent into crime.

Computer, arcade games and violence

If watching television may encourage aggressive behaviour, what about video or arcade games which are interactive and so give the child the opportunity to participate in a representation of an aggressive activity? Bestsellers such as *Sonic the Hedgehog*, *Super Mario*, *Mortal Kombat* and *Streetfighter* involve fighting and other aggressive activities to reach their goal. *Doom*, *Resident Evil*, *Crazy Taxi*, *Grand Theft Auto* and *Carmageddon* reward players for the numbers that can be gunned down, run down or battered into submission. In *Carmageddon*, the aim is to score points by running down pedestrians and animals. In an American study, Schutte et al. (1988) had male and female, 5- to 7-year-old children play either *Karateka* (a game where villains must be hit or kicked in order for the hero to reach the target) or *Jungle Hunt* (a non-violent game where the hero swings through trees to reach the target). Those playing *Karateka* were found to be much more likely to hit both their playmate and a Bobo doll than those who had played *Jungle Hunt*.

The computer game *Phantasmagoria* is described as 'a chilling psychological thriller' which contains so many images of violence and torture that it has a special 'gore button' allowing parents to cut out the most blood-thirsty scenes.

Not only is concern raised about video games, but there is growing concern about multimedia personal computers. In the December 1995 issue of *Which?* consumer magazine there is a report on an issue of *The Mac* computer magazine which gave a free CD-Rom carrying an excerpt from *Voyeur*, apparently 'a sexy adult thriller', a game which carries an 18 rating from the British Board of Film Classification. The concern of *Which?* magazine is that there are no age restrictions on who can buy *The Mac* magazine (and therefore obtain the free disc).

The effects of watching television violence

How does watching violence on television, videotape or computer game influence people? There are five suggested effects:

1 *Imitation:* watching violent television might lead to imitation, and observers may well act out what they have seen. The tragic real-life events outlined above clearly demonstrate that imitation does

happen. One example is that of Michael Ryan who shot and killed many people in the village of Hungerford. Numerous videotapes depicting violence were later discovered at his home. It is argued that exposure to media violence provides viewers with new ideas and techniques of aggressing to which they were previously oblivious.

2 *Disinhibition*: people's inhibitions or restraints are reduced as violence becomes a part of their everyday life.

3 *Desensitisation*: refers to our decreased sensitivity to stimuli that are presented constantly over a period of time; our gradual emotional desensitisation to pain or suffering in others. This means that a viewer who watches too much television violence becomes adapted to it and further violence becomes less objectionable.

4 *Arousal*: for those not desensitised, watching a violent programme is likely to increase their level of physiological arousal. Although this may not lead to the performance of aggressive behaviour immediately afterwards, the arousal may be transferred to some other situation after a period of time (this is excitation transfer; see Chapter 7). However, those who watch a large amount of television (and become desensitised) may show a less emotional response.

5 *New cognitions*: repeated exposure to violence could lead us to perceive future information in terms of aggressive intent where aggression was not intended. Huesmann (1988) suggests that exposure to violence can create aggression-related scripts (a cognition of how to behave should the situation arise). So, if children find themselves in a similar situation to the one they observed they will behave according to the violent script rather than seek alternative solutions.

The extent of the problem

Is the situation as bad as is being made out? Is there violence on television every time we switch on? Just how much violence is there on television? Another question demanding an answer is whether viewers consider what they watch is actually violent. Can children distinguish between fantasy and reality? Are children's cartoons a problem? We consider each of these questions in turn.

How much violence is actually shown on television?

Rather than include every violent act, Cumberbatch (1987) defines television violence as 'any action of physical force with or without a weapon against oneself or another person, animal or inanimate object, whether carried through or merely attempted and whether the action caused injury or not'.

From work in the United States it has been found that there was an average of eight acts of violence per hour and in children's cartoons a violent act occurred every two minutes. In Britain the BBC's Audience Research Department began studies in 1972 leading to a large-scale study supervised by Cumberbatch in 1977. This British study found significantly less violence. Taking into account all forms of violence, there were just 1.68 violent acts per hour, rising to only 1.96 acts when verbal threats were included. Such data are taken as being as accurate as they can be in that they covered four channels: BBC1; BBC2; ITV; and Channel Four on four separate weeks amounting, to 1,412 hours and some 2,076 programmes being surveyed.

In recent years, however, there has been a significant increase in the different types of television: cable and satellite in addition to terrestrial networks. Whereas terrestrial channels are governed by the 9 p.m. 'watershed', encrypted channels have a little more freedom. As discovered by Clarke (1996), on Sky Movies for Sunday 3 December 1995 between 8 a.m. and 8 p.m. of the six films shown, five had a PG (parental guidance) certificate. Whereas American cartoons, often with a high violence content, once comprised a very small percentage of viewing time on terrestrial channels, the birth of The Disney Channel and The Cartoon Network (on cable/satellite from 5 a.m. to 9 p.m.) has provided children with non-stop opportunities to observe violent acts.

What viewers consider as violence

According to Cumberbatch (1987) there is a difference between what researchers and viewers perceive as violence. He suggests that viewers, particularly children, can be highly discriminating. Children know that some programmes are violent but that by the end of the programme no one will have got hurt and so it is not real violence. Barwise and Ehrenberg (1994) believe that many children loved watching the

A Team and did not find it at all disturbing because they knew that no one was hurt. They further suggest that the characters and the predictably happy ending were all reassuring, somewhat like the happy ending of a frightening fairy tale. Conversely, it is argued that this is precisely the problem: children may well copy a violent act demonstrated by their heroes, making the assumption that it is harmless when in fact it may have disastrous consequences.

What about parents? Do they consider programmes such as the *A Team* to be violent? Messenger-Davies (1989) discovered that although most parents (60 per cent) thought that watching violent television made children more aggressive, 75 per cent thought that *Magnum*, *Minder* and the *A Team* were harmless even for those under 5 years of age.

A further example of children showing discrimination between real violence and 'pretend' violence can be found through their views on cartoons. Gerbner et al. (1980) found that cartoons contain the most violence of any television programme: of the ninety-five cartoons analysed only one did not contain violence. However, children see cartoons as containing hardly any violence at all, considering them not to be a true reflection of reality. The difference may be between what children say and what children do, or that they were confused by a question. This could well explain why, despite saying that cartoons are not real violence, studies show that cartoons do lead children to behave aggressively. For example, Ellis and Sekgra (1972) showed children either an aggressive cartoon (with incidents of aggression in a football match) or a neutral cartoon (a song and dance routine). Later, in the classroom, those who had seen the violent cartoon behaved much more aggressively.

Conclusions

The conclusion from a large number of studies is that although observing violence on television may be a contributory factor to aggressive behaviour, it does not follow automatically. Other factors may be equally, if not more influential. Working in the United States, Eron (1982) concludes that watching television violence is one cause of aggression in children, but the joint occurrence of several factors determines how violent a young person becomes. Similarly, Durkin (1985) argues against Bandura's 'hypodermic' model – the idea that what goes in automatically comes out again in the same form. Durkin suggests that the children's own personalities and aspirations affect their viewing tastes. Messenger-Davies (1989), for instance, believes that 'What children get from television depends on what children bring to it. Depending on how old they are, how bright they are, how tired they are, what sort of family they belong to, what sort of skills they already have, television will affect them differently.' The important question which remains unanswered is: does television make children violent or do children who are already violent choose to watch violent television?

What can be done?

There are a number of possibilities:

- Parents can help: if a child watches violence in the presence of an adult who condemns the violence the child is less likely to behave aggressively.
- Parents can also help if children are encouraged to discriminate between fantasy and real-life events, by discussing how special effects are used to simulate violence.
- Parents can help by enforcing strict limits on the amount of television watched: ensuring children do not watch 'late-night' television (i.e. after 9 p.m.); ensuring children do not watch 'video nasties'.
- Impose limits on those who make programmes: in February 2001 TV regulators (the Independent Television Commission) ruled that risqué scenes (in programmes such as *The Jerry Springer Show* and *Trisha*) must not be shown on daytime programmes during school holidays. However, whilst ITV had complied, satellite channels ITV2 and Living had not.
- Reverse the trend and introduce more educational programmes: Huesmann et al. (1988) taught 170 children that: television violence is unrealistic; most people do not behave aggressively; the average person finds alternative solutions; watching television violence is undesirable; children should not imitate the violence they see. By the end of the second year of the study the experimental participants were judged to be less aggressive than the control group who had received no training.

- What about the people who write, produce and distribute violent films aimed at children? What are they going to do about it? The answer is very little, simply because they argue that they are responding to the demands of the public and they are making money from it.
- What about people who write computer software such as *Carmageddon*? One response, from the director of a leading software company, is that all the research they know about concludes that there is not a problem!

Summary

Many studies have shown that children imitate models they have observed. This has implications because we wish children not to copy anti-social behaviours but to copy pro-social behaviours. Television plays a significant role and the evidence for the effects of television on behaviour presented in this chapter is divided into four categories: laboratory studies, field studies, longitudinal studies and cross-cultural studies. Alternative media are also considered, such as videotape, arcade and computer games and how their content can lead to an increase in anti-social behaviours. It is possible to counteract the effect of anti-social behaviour in the media in two main ways: by limiting the number of anti-social programmes available for viewing and to increase the number of pro-social programmes.

Essay question: Discuss the view that the media might influence anti-social behaviour.

Review exercise

Further reading

Fowles, J. (1999) *The Case for Television Violence*. Sage Publications.

Gunter, B. and Harrison, J. (1998) *Violence on Television*. Routledge. Both these texts provide much food for thought regarding the television and violence debate.

Messenger-Davies, M. (1989) *Television is Good for your Kids*. Hilary Shipman Ltd. Very readable account of various aspects of television, particularly for enhancing pro-social behaviours.

11

Study aids

IMPROVING YOUR ESSAY WRITING SKILLS

At this point in the book you have acquired the knowledge necessary to tackle the exam itself. Answering exam questions is a skill and in this chapter we hope to help you improve this skill. By studying the essays presented in this chapter, and the examiner's comments, you can learn how to improve your essays and examination answers. Please note that marks given by the examiner in the practice essays should be used as a guide only and are not definitive. They represent the raw marks given by an AQA(A) examiner: that is, the marks the examiner would give to the Examining Board based on a total of 24 marks per question broken down into Skill A01 (description) and Skill A02 (evaluation). A table showing this scheme is in the Appendix of Paul Humphreys' title in this series, *Exam Successes in AEB Psychology*.

The marks given will not be the same as on an examination results slip received ultimately by the student because all examining boards are required to use a common standardised system called the Uniform Mark Scale (UMS). This adjusts all raw scores to a single standard acceptable to all Examining Boards.

In writing AQA(A) examination answers, students can usually improve if they avoid making the following common errors:

- Failing to answer the specific question set; instead writing the 'Blue Peter' answer which they prepared earlier, and hoping that it will do.
- Similarly, writing all they know on a topic rather than selecting from what they know to fit the question.
- In writing all they know they describe far too much (Skill A01) at the expense of evaluation (Skill A02), producing an imbalanced answer.
- Writing too much (and so spending too much time) on one answer at the expense of others.

The essays which follow are about the length a student would be able to write in about twenty-five minutes (leaving a little extra time for planning and checking). Each essay is followed by detailed comments about its strengths and weaknesses. When you look through the essays, ask yourself if the answer suffers from any of the common problems outlined above or whether the answer is balanced, has appropriate length and answers the question set. Also bear in mind that the 'perfect answer' should be coherent, logically organised and have good use of spelling, punctuation and grammar.

For more ideas on how to write good essays, you should consult *Exam Successes in AEB Psychology* by Paul Humphreys in this series.

Practice essay 1

Describe and evaluate psychological research relating to human altruism and/or bystander behaviour. AEB (now AQA[A]) June 1998

Examiner's advice

Starting point – *A good point to start is with the words 'describe' and 'evaluate'. The injunction 'describe' requires you to present evidence of your knowledge of the stipulated topic area (in this case human altruism and/or bystander behaviour). The term 'evaluate' requires you to make an informed judgement regarding the value of the evidence presented, based on a systematic analysis and examination of it. In this respect, the description is Skill A01 (knowledge-based and descriptive skills) and evaluation is Skill A02 (analytical and* *evaluative skills). For this question, as these two skills are explicitly required, candidates should present an answer which has a roughly equal balance of each. It should also be noted that candidates can consider human altruism, or bystander behaviour or a combination of the two, allowing a little more flexibility. Further, the question does specify human altruism, and so description of non-human altruism would receive no credit for Skill A01. It could, however, be used for evaluation (Skill A02). It is also worth noting that the word 'research' indicates the need for both theories **and** studies on the stipulated area.*

Candidate's answer

Latané and Darley (1970) researched bystander behaviour in their epileptic seizure experiment. This was inspired by news stories of people not helping others in situations where it would seem implausible not to help. In their experiment, participants were in separate booths but they could hear each other. There was a condition in which there were two participants (but one was a confederate), in the next condition there were two real participants and a confederate and in the next there were six real participants and one confederate. The participants did not know the nature of the experiment. In each case, the confederate would call out that he was having an epileptic seizure. Participants' reaction time in helping was recorded. It was found that even the presence of one other non-epileptic dramatically increased the time taken to respond, and in the third condition, participants took a long time to provide help.

Latané and Darley next decided to investigate whether people would save themselves, by their 'smoke-filled room' experiment, in which participants in a waiting room found smoke pouring into the room. The same effects were found and in a condition in which the experimenter was in the room only one participant took any action!

Thus both these experiments show clear evidence of bystander behaviour and it was concluded that bystander behaviour can occur for three reasons: first because of audience inhibition, where the person is embarrassed to act in front of others, especially if their opinion is valued; second pluralistic ignorance can occur, in which everyone assumes that other people know best what to do and look to others to see what should be done, and thus, if no one else is helping, people do not help either; third there is diffusion of responsibility, so if there are ten other bystanders one might think it is not their responsibility because there are all these other people.

The Latané and Darley experiments described were both laboratory experiments and so could be criticised for artificiality. Piliavin et al. decided to conduct an experiment in the real world (1981) and so conducted the 'subway study'. This study involved an actor collapsing on a subway train. He either appeared drunk and clutched a bottle with a brown paper bag, or appeared ill and clutched a cane. He was either black or white. Piliavin found that the race of the victim made no difference to the likelihood or reaction time of help. They did find, however, that bystanders were less likely to help the 'drunk' person than the 'ill' person.

Another real-world investigation was into a person who drops their books in a lift. Here the 'diffusion of responsibility' idea was enacted clearly, with helpfulness decreasing as the number of bystanders increased.

Altruism is when someone helps someone else for no reason of gain to themselves. An example of a theory of altruism is the Darwin theory that altruism evolved. Wilson 1975 says that we have altruism 'programmed into our genes'. Helping others at the expense of our-selves is evolutionarily known as the paradox of altruism. However, we do aid the furtherance of our genes by helping those who also carry our genes, ideally someone younger and fitter. It has been found that people are more likely to help those who look like themselves. However, this could also be attributed to the empathy–altrusim model, by Batson (1991), who claims that we help others because we imagine what it must feel like for them.

Bierhoff claims to have found an actual 'helping personality' by research – the person would feel socially responsible, believe in a just world, and have an internal locus of control.

Social learning theorists have researched altruism: for example Midlarsky et al. found that the best way to make a child learn to be helpful is to show them a behaviour and then to reward them when they copy it. However, this has more to do with learning than real altruism.

Research has shown that people will be more likely to allow themselves to be more altruistic if they possess the necessary skills to help the person in need (Clark and Word). This could be related to bystander behaviour – people don't if they don't know what to do. Maruyama suggests that people stand by if they are seen with someone they see as a leader.

There is much research to suggest that people do not act because of altruism out of self-serving motives. It has been shown that people are more likely to help if there are others present who will disapprove if they don't help (Piliavin) or if they will be rewarded.

Research has shown that people are more likely to display altruistic behaviour towards those who are attractive, who are weak and help-less and who bear resemblance to the helper. This research could be taken to support evolutionary theories of altruism. However, why do people risk their lives to save their dogs or other people's children? This could also be taken to support empathy–altruism as people could empathise better with those who are 'like' them. Altruism is hard to prove because there is so much research which suggests that people help for difference reasons.

Examiner's comment

The candidate launches into describing Latané and Darley's 'epileptic seizure' study without any introduction or explanation of what the study relates to. He/she then stops and comments on what led to this study being performed, namely news stories of people not helping. It is worth commenting here that a significant number of candidates spend time describing in ample detail the tragic Kitty Genovese incident. Whilst this study could be mentioned, it is worth keeping the detail to no more than a sentence or two. The candidate then describes in reasonably accurate detail the 'epileptic seizure' study. The second paragraph describes yet another Latané and Darley laboratory study, that of the 'smoke-filled room experiment'. The candidate exhibits good style here, because rather than explain the results in full, the comment 'the same effects were found' is used.

So far the candidate has shown evidence of description and knowledge (Skill A01). The start of the third paragraph is where he/she shows clear understanding when the summary statement brings the evidence together. The three reasons for bystander behaviour that follow are clear, concise and accurate. So far, no Skill A02 is evident.

In the fourth paragraph the candidate begins to show Skill A02 in the comment about artificiality and then introducing Piliavin as an alternative to laboratory evidence. This is good contrast of evidence but, crucially, the candidate does not make it clear that whereas diffusion of responsibility was found in the laboratory studies, it was not found in the field study.

In paragraph six, the candidate has made the decision to say no more about bystander effects and to concentrate on altruism. Remember the question specified human *altruism. The candidate begins this paragraph with a definition of altruism. Although she/he does not give a name and date for the quote (names and dates are desirable though not essential) the candidate's understanding of altruism is evident. The following description is good, with the candidate using terms that clearly apply to humans. Skill A02 evaluation is also evident at the end of this paragraph.*

In the next paragraph the candidate introduces the work of Batson, but disappointingly does not have more than a sentence of description. The work of Bierhoff is then introduced to further the point that people help because they want to. A comment is also made about the work of Midlarsky which is evaluated with the last sentence of the paragraph. Yet further research is introduced in relation to altruism with the point being made that this could well apply to bystander behaviour too. Points like this are good because they show understanding of the concepts involved. The remainder of the answer is entirely Skill A02. First the candidate makes a comment that research has shown that people help not because of altruism but for other reasons. In the final paragraph the answer includes a summary where again evaluative points are made.

Overall this is a good answer that considers both bystander behaviour and altruism. Quite a wide range of studies are covered, some described in more detail than others. Some theories are considered, those explaining bystander behaviour and altruism, with again, some described in more detail than others. If this essay is marked out of 24 marks, with 12 marks for skill A01 and 12 marks for Skill A02, this answer would attract 10 marks out of 12 for Skill A01 and 8 out of 12 for Skill A02, giving an overall mark of 18/24 – equivalent to a grade A.

Practice essay 2

'One of the achievements of social psychology has been in extending explanations of aggression and violence away from merely being reflection to demonstrate ways of the inner state of individuals' (Howitt et al. 1989). With reference to the issues in the above quotation, critically consider the view that aggression can be explained in social psychological terms. (24 marks) AEB (now AQA [A]) January 1998.

Examiner's advice

Starting point – *A good point to start is with the words 'critically consider'. The injunction 'consider' requires you to demonstrate your knowledge and understanding of the stipulated topic area (in this case social psychological explanations of aggression). The term 'critically' requires you to show an awareness of the strengths and limitations of the evidence presented. In this respect, the consideration is Skill A01 (knowledge-based and descriptive skills) and the 'critical' aspect is Skill A02 (analytical and evaluative skills). For this question, as these two skills are explicitly required, candidates should present an answer which has a roughly equal balance of each. It should also be noted that candidates are not required to describe non-social theories but these can be credited if they are presented as alternatives to social-psychological theories.*

Candidate's answer

Aggression is a behaviour which is intended to harm someone psychologically or physically. Past research suggested that aggression and violence were 'reflections of the inner state of individuals' as quoted by Howitt et al. 1989. This quote suggests violence and aggression were due to the individual's personality and, as Lorenz believed, aggression is instinctive in all species: ethological approach.

Social psychology recently has found other possible answers to explain aggression which consider situational effects that may explain aggression and violence in the social learning theory – as proposed by Bandura in the 1960s. Bandura believed that aggression was imitated through observation of role models, particularly in children. Bandura showed this in a study in 1966 whereby schoolchildren were placed in a room with an adult role model acting aggressively toward the bobo doll, punching and kicking it. When the model left the room the children were observed. The results showed that the children imitated the model's behaviour and continued to kick and punch the bobo doll when the model had left: imitation. Bandura also found that the model's behaviour was more likely to be imitated if the aggressive behaviour was rewarded, and less likely to be imitated if the behaviour was punished.

However, this study has been criticised for a number of reasons. First, the study was very artificial and demand characteristics could have occurred. The children were in an unusual situation with these dolls; therefore the children may have believed it was expected that the aggressive behaviour should be shown. The behaviour towards the doll may also have been considered appropriate by the children as this behaviour is considered appropriate in other situations, for example sport.

Bandura also claimed that the role model influenced the child imitating behaviour. Bandura believed that the boys were more likely to imitate other male models. Similarity between the child and model was of importance; the more similar the child was to the model; the more likely the child would imitate the model. This social learning theory therefore is an alternative social psychological method of explaining aggression and violence, other than it merely being a 'reflection of the inner state of individuals'.

Another social psychological theory which explains aggression and violence in terms of situational effects is Berkowitz's cue-dependent theory. Berkowitz believed that aggressive or violent behaviour was the result of environmental stimuli rather than a 'reflection of the inner state of individuals'. Berkowitz said certain people or objects caused frustration which led to anger. For this anger to lead to aggression certain cues are needed, such as objects, as the following studies demonstrate.

Berkowitz had a number of participants who were placed into pairs: individual A and individual B. Individual A had to provide a written solution to a problem. Individual B then evaluated the solution and gave electric shocks to the individual depending upon the solution. One shock meant the solution was favourable and up to 10+ shocks for an unfavourable solution. Individual A was then shown either a violent or non-violent film and then this person evaluated the other individual's solution, in terms of shocks. The results showed that the more shocks were given if the participant had viewed a violent film. These results therefore suggest that the cue, a violent film, led to an increase in aggressive behaviour.

Another study in 1967 was done by Berkowitz whereby after the participant had viewed the non-violent aggressive film, they were taken to a control room where had been placed badminton racquets, or a revolver or nothing on the table. These were the cues. The results showed that when there were aggressive cues (revolver), more shocks were given to another individual. Less shocks were given when there were neutral objects or non-aggressive objects such as 'badminton racquets' or no objects. Berkowitz named this the 'weapons effect' where an aggressive object merely being in the room caused more shocks to be given by the individual.

This therefore supports the social-psychological theory that situational effects do result in aggression and therefore explain aggression as well as theories such as instinctive theories (Lorenz) where aggression merely reflects 'the inner state of individuals'. However, such studies above which support the cue-related theory have been criticised for reasons such as the situation being artificial. The person in the control room told the participant that the objects must have been left by an individual from the last study; however, demand characteristics may have occurred.

Aggression can therefore be explained in social-psychological terms which consider situational effects rather than just 'reflections of the inner state of individuals'.

Examiner's comment

The candidate begins by providing a simple definition of aggression and then immediately addresses the quote contained in the question by looking at how the quote concerns individuals whereas the area to be considered, social psychological theories, does not. This is a good beginning as it sets out exactly what the gist of the question is, what is and what is not the focus of the question, and it shows understanding.

In the second paragraph the candidate begins to look at social learning theory as the first of the social-psychological theories to be included. The focus is the work of Bandura and his original 'bobo doll' study. Description here is quite good and what happened in the study is clear (Skill A01). In the third paragraph the candidate evaluated the Bandura study (Skill A02). A number of appropriate points are made but are superficial.

In the next paragraph the candidate considers some additional research conducted by Bandura and concludes the section with a comment about how what has been said relates to the quote. It is worth noting that in questions where a quote is included, it is important that answers address the issues raised in the quote. To help remind candidates to do this, the question does state 'with reference to the quote'. The candidate then introduces the next social-psychological theory which is the effect of situational factors on aggression. He/she outlines the 'cue-dependent' theory of Berkowitz, which is then nicely linked to the frustration-aggression hypothesis. Two studies performed by Berkowitz are then considered and a good amount of description is included. The candidate shows good analysis and understanding when using comments such as 'this therefore supports the social-psychological theory'. At this point reference is made again to the quote and a reference to why such theories are in opposition to Lorenz. A few sentences of evaluation in relation to the Berkowitz studies are then made but these are very brief and lack depth. The candidate ends the answer by again referring to the quote.

Overall this is a good answer that considers two appropriate social psychological theories of aggression. The candidate has decided to go for detail (depth) rather than range (breadth), and in the top band answer both these components should be balanced. There is some attempt to consider critically but this is quite limited and restricted mainly to the Bandura studies. If this answer is marked out of 24, with 12 marks allocated for Skill A01 and 12 marks for Skill A02, this answer will attract 9 marks out of 12 for Skill A01 and 6 out of 12 for Skill A02, giving an overall mark of 15/24. This would be equivalent to a grade B.

Glossary

The first occurrence of each of these terms is highlighted in bold type in the main text.

Aggressive crowd a crowd or mob whose intent is aggressive.

Aggression machine a machine which, when operated, appears to deliver electric shocks to a 'victim'. A way of measuring a person's aggression.

Altruism helping which is motivated purely out of concern for others' well-being, and not motivated by self-interest.

Anti-social describing behaviour or tendencies which are contrary to the benefit of society e.g. aggression, criminal activity, etc.

Appeasement gestures a submissive gesture adopted by an animal to show admission of defeat to its opponent.

Audience inhibition the effect of people deciding not to help as a result of onlooking bystanders, because of their fear that their incompetence in the task will actually increase as a result of having an audience. Opposite of social facilitation effect (q.v.).

Cognitive neo-associationism describes the model proposed by Berkowitz 1989 which states that a person decides whether to stay and become aggressive or leave depending on their cognitive appraisal of the situation and the social norms that apply.

Collectivist cultures typically found in non-industrialised countries.

Cultures based on a view emphasising co-operation, community and family values. Opposite of individualist cultures (q.v.).

Cumulative continuity the tendency of an individual to choose environments and friends which help sustain their aggressive predisposition.

Deindividuation the process whereby a person loses individuality and personal accountability when part of a group, leading to anti-social behaviour.

Demand characteristics cues which participants pick up on which may then affect their behaviour in favour of the experimental aim.

Ecological validity the extent to which the procedure and setting of research is like real life.

Egoism self-interest, e.g. helping purely to benefit oneself in some way, rather than the person being helped.

Empathic-joy hypothesis the idea that we are motivated to help both out of empathy for 'the victim' as well as expectation of experiencing happiness or joy as a result of such an action.

Empathy the state of vicariously experiencing another person's emotions.

Empathy–altruism hypothesis explanation of helping behaviour. Empathy motivates people to reduce the distress of the person in need by helping them.

Environmental determinism the view that aspects of the environment (e.g. noise or crowding) cause specific behaviours, e.g. heat causes riots hypothesis.

Environmental possibilism the view that environmental factors may exert a small influence on our behaviour.

Environmental probabilism the view that environmental factors probably exert some influence on our behaviour.

Excitation transfer theory proposed by Zillmann 1971. The theory explains aggressive behaviour as a result of two stages; first, a person becomes physiologically aroused (the 'excitation'), a state which may linger for some time; second, another event causing mild frustration facilitates the release of the aggression. Hence the original excitation may be transferred to another situation.

Freedom the idea that our behaviour is freely chosen; that we exercise free will, rather than our behaviour being determined by forces beyond our control. (See environmental determinism and genetic determinism.)

Frustration the emotion experienced when goal-directed behaviour is blocked.

Genetic determinism the view that our behaviour and personality is determined by our genes.

Genotype a group of organisms of the same genetic constitution.

Hostile aggression an act of aggression with the intent of inflicting pain.

Inclusive fitness evolutionary concept. Individuals are not just motivated to ensure own genetic survival, but also survival of those sharing a similar genetic make-up.

Incompatible responses the idea that it is not possible to act on two contrary or incompatible emotions at the same time, e.g. empathy and aggression.

Individualist cultures usually found in industrialised countries. Cultures based on a view emphasising individuality, uniqueness, difference and competition.

Instrumental aggression an act of aggression with some other goal than that of inflicting pain, e.g. shoving someone out of the way in order to get out of a dangerous situation.

Interactional continuity when an individual should choose environments and friends which help to counteract their aggressive pre-disposition

Inter-species aggression aggressive acts that take place between individuals of different species.

Intra-species aggression aggressive acts that take place between individuals of the same species.

'Just-world' hypothesis the idea that people get what they deserve; that good things happen to good people and the reverse for bad people. Could be a justification for not helping somebody.

Nature–nurture debate the long-held debate concerning whether personality and behaviour is learnt ('nurture') or is genetically determined ('nature').

Negative affect technical term for unpleasant feelings such as sadness, irritability or self-loathing.

Negative state relief model model proposed by Cialdini that explains the motivation for helping as a way of relieving the negative state (physiological arousal) brought about by witnessing an emergency situation.

Personalised norms an individual's own feelings of moral obligation and standards of behaviour. Relates to Schwartz's Theory of norm activation.

Primary territory an area usually owned and used by an individual or group (e.g. home or car or nest) which people try to protect from invasion or infringement.

Pro-social behaviour describing any behaviour which is positive for society, e.g. conformity, co-operation, helping, etc.

Reciprocal altruism an apparently altruistic act for another individual may later be returned, hence benefiting both individuals and increasing their likelihood of survival.

Reciprocity norm where we feel morally obliged to help those who have helped us in the past: 'you scratch my back and I'll scratch yours'.

Ritualised fighting aggression, usually shown in animals, which is not harmful but is usually a set series of threat displays culminating in an appeasement or submissive gesture.

Sanctioned aggression aggression which is 'approved of' by the state, e.g. police shooting an armed bank-robber.

Self-serving bias way of interpreting own and others' behaviour, attributing the cause of behaviour to make oneself appear in a good light.

Shock-competition technique technique for measuring aggression in the laboratory involving two people giving each other electric shocks using aggression machines (q.v.).

Shock-learning technique laboratory method for measuring aggression. Participants, using fake electric shock generating machinery, ostensibly give electric shocks to another person (usually a stooge) for failures in a learning task. Aggression measured by number of shocks delivered and/or intensity of the shocks.

Social facilitation effect opposite of audience inhibition. When a person is competent in a certain skill, having an audience actually increases their performance in that type of task.

Social loafing phenomenon whereby the more people are present, the lazier each individual becomes, putting less effort into the current task.

Socialised norms accepted ways of behaving and responding to situations which are acquired through socialisation and growing up.

Social responsibility norm erroneous idea proposed by Berkowitz and Daniels that we help those in need precisely because they need us / they are dependent upon us.

Sociobiology a subject that works on the premise that social behaviour is biologically / genetically determined and that this behaviour has been selected through the process of evolution and selection.

Stimulus overload theory idea to explain the apparent lower degree of helping in urban areas: city dwellers frequently encounter emergency situations and so pay less attention to such situations and hence are less likely to respond pro-socially.

Threat displays usually used to describe animal gestures, often stereotyped actions performed to indicate aggressive intent without actually inflicting harm.

Type A behaviour behaviour that is characterised by a high level of competition, motivation, time pressure and aggression.

Weapons effect theory propounded by Berkowitz explaining aggression as a function of availability of weapons, i.e. if a person has access to a weapon, when frustrated the weapon acts as a cue, triggering or suggesting aggressive behaviour, even though the weapon itself may not be used.

References

Aiello, J.R., Nicosia, G.J. and Thompson, D.E. (1979) Physiological, social and behavioural consequences of crowding on children and adolescents. *Child Development* 50, 195–202.

Ainsworth, P.B. and Pease, K. (1987) *Police Work*. The British Psychological Society/Methuen.

Altman, D. (1969) Trust of the stranger in the city and the small town. Unpublished research, City University of New York.

Amato, P.R. (1983) Helping behaviour in urban and rural environments: field studies based on taxonomic organisation of helping episodes. *Journal of Personality and Social Psychology* 45, 571–586.

Anderson, C.A. (1989) Temperature and aggression: ubiquitous effects of heat on occurrence of human violence. *Psychological Bulletin* 106, 74–96.

Archer, D. (1994) American violence: how high and why? *Law Studies* 19, 2–20.

Archer, D. and Gartner, R. (1976) Violent acts and violent times; a comparative approach to post-war homicide rates. *American Sociological Review* 41, 937–963.

Arms, R.L., Russell, G.W. and Sandilands, M.L. (1980) Effects of viewing aggressive sports on the hostility of spectators. In R.M. Suinn (ed.) *Psychology in Sports: Methods and Applications*. Minneapolis: Burgess Publishing Co.

Aronson, E., Wilson, T.D. and Akert, R.M. (1999) *Social Psychology*, 3rd edn. Harlow: Longman.

Bandura, A. (1965) Influence of a model's reinforcement contingencies on the acquisition of imitative responses. *Journal of Personality and Social Psychology* 1, 589–595.

Bandura, A. (1977) *Social Learning Theory*. Englewood Cliffs, NJ: Prentice-Hall.

Bandura, A. (1986) *Social Foundations of Thought and Action: A Social Cognitive Theory*. Englewood Cliffs, NJ: Prentice-Hall.

Bandura, A., Ross, D. and Ross, S.A. (1961) Transmission of aggression through imitation of aggressive models. *Journal of Abnormal and Social Psychology* 63, 575–582.

Banyard, P. and Grayson, A. (1996) *Introducing Psychological Research*. Basingstoke: Macmillan.

Baran, S.J. (1979) Television drama as a facilitator of pro-social behaviour. *Journal of Broadcast* 23, 277–285.

Barker, R., Dembo, T. and Lewin, K. (1941) Frustration and aggression: an experiment with young children. *University of Iowa Studies in Child Welfare* 18, 1–314.

Baron, R.A. (1974) The aggression-inhibiting influence of heightened sexual arousal. *Journal of Personality and Social Psychology* 30, 318–322.

Baron, R.A. (1980) Olfaction and human social behaviour: effects of pleasant scents on physical aggression. *Basic and Applied Social Psychology* 1, 163–172.

Baron, R.A. (1997) The sweet smell of . . . helping: effects of pleasant ambient fragrance on pro-social behaviour in shopping malls. *Personality and Social Psychology Bulletin* 23, 498–503.

Baron, R.A. and Bell, P.A. (1977) Sexual arousal and aggression by males: type of erotic stimuli and prior provocation. *Journal of personality and social psychology* 35, 79–87.

Baron, R.A. and Ransberger, V.M. (1978) Ambient temperature and the occurrence of collective violence: the 'long hot summer' revisited. *Journal of Personality and Social Psychology* 36, 351–360.

Baron, R.A. and Byrne, D. (1994) *Social Psychology*, 7th edn. London: Allyn & Bacon.

Barwise P. and Ehrenberg, A. (1988) *Television and its Audience*. London: Sage.

Batson, C.D. (1991) *The Altruism Question: Toward a Social-psychological Answer*. Hillsdale, NJ: Erlbaum.

Batson, C.D. (1998) Altruism and prosocial behaviour. In D. Gilbert (ed.) *The Handbook of Social Psychology*, 4th edn., New York: McGraw-Hill, vol. 2, pp. 282–316.

Batson, C.D., Duncan, B.D., Ackerman, P., Buckley, T. and Birch, K. (1981) Is empathic emotion a source of altruistic motivation? *Journal of Personality and Social Psychology* 40, 290–302.

Batson, C.D., Oleson, K.C., Weeks, J.L., Healey, S.P., Reeves, P.J., Jennings, P. and Brown, T. (1989) Religious prosocial motivation: is it altruistic or egoistic? *Journal of Personality and Social Psychology* 57, 873–884.

Beaman, A.L., Barnes, P.J., Klentz, B. and McQuirk, B. (1978) Increasing helping rates through information dissemination: teaching pays. *Personality and Social Psychology Bulletin* 4, 406–411.

Berkowitz, L. (1970) Experimental investigations of hostility catharsis. *Journal of Consulting and Clinical Psychology* 35, 1–7.

Berkowitz, L. (1989) Frustration-aggression hypothesis: examination and reformulation. *Psychological Bulletin* 106, 59–73.

Berkowitz, L., and Daniels, L.R. (1963) Responsibility and dependency. *Journal of Abnormal and Social Psychology* 66, 429–437.

Berkowitz, L. and Geen, R. (1966) Film violence and the cue properties of available targets. *Journal of Personality and Social Psychology* 3, 525–530.

Berkowitz, L. and LePage, A. (1967) Weapons as aggression-eliciting stimuli. *Journal of Personality and Social Psychology* 11, 202–207.

Bickman, L. (1972) Social influence and diffusion of responsibility in an emergency. *Journal of Experimental Social Psychology* 8, 438–445.

Bierhoff, H.W., Klein, R. and Kramp, P. (1991) Evidence for the altruistic personality from data on accident research. *Journal of Personality* 59, 263–280.

Bower, G.H. and Hilgard, E.R. (1981) *Theories of Learning* (5th edn) Englewood Cliffs, NJ: Prentice Hall.

Brown, P. and Elliot, R. (1965) Control of aggression in a nursery school class. *Journal of Experimental Child Psychology* 2, 103–107.

Bryan, J.H. and Test, M.A. (1967) Models and helping: naturalistic studies in aiding behaviour. *Journal of Personality and Social Psychology* 6, 400–407.

Bryant, B.K. (1982) An index of empathy for children and adolescents. *Child Development* 53, 413–425.

Bryant, J. and Zillmann, D. (1979) Effect of intensification of annoyance through unrelated residual excitation on substantially delayed hostile behaviour. *Journal of Experimental Social Psychology* 15, 470–480.

Burnstein, E., Crandall, C. and Kitayama, S. (1994) Some neo-Darwin decision rules for altruism: weighing cues for inclusive fitness as a function of the biological importance of the decision. *Journal of Personality and Social Psychology* 67, 773–789.

Buss, A. (1963) Physical aggression in relation to different frustrations. *Journal of Abnormal and Social Psychology* 67, 1–7.

Caspi, A., Bem, D.J. and Elder, G.H. (1989) Continuities and consequences of interactional styles across the life course. *Journal of Personality* 57, 375–406.

Cialdini, R.B., Baumann, D.J. and Kenrick, D.T. (1981) Insights from sadness: a three-step model of the development of altruism as hedonism. *Development Review* 1, 207–223.

Cialdini, R.B., Kenrick, D.T. and Hoerig, J.H. (1976) Victim derogation in the learner paradigm: just world or just justification? *Journal of Personality and Social Psychology* 33, 719–724.

Cialdini, R.B., Schaller, M., Houlainhan, D., Arps, K., Fultz, J. and Beaman, A.L. (1987) Empathy-based helping: is it selflessly or selfishly motivated? *Journal of Personality and Social Psychology* 52, 749–758.

Clark, R.D. and Word, L.E. (1972) Why don't bystanders help? Because of ambiguity? *Journal of Personality and Social Psychology* 24, 392–400.

Clark, R.D. and Word, L.E. (1974) Where is the apathetic bystander? Situational characteristics of the emergency. *Journal of Personality and Social Psychology* 29, 279–287.

Clarke, D.J. (1996) Social influence. Chapter 3 in M. Cardwell, L. Clark and C. Meldrum (eds), *Psychology for A Level*. London: Harper Collins.

Coke, J.S., Batson, C.D. and McDavis, K. (1978) Empathic mediation of helping: a two-stage model. *Journal of Personality and Social Psychology* 36, 752–766.

Cox, V.C., Paulus, P.B. and McCain, G. (1984) Prison crowding research. *American Psychologist* 39, 1148–1160.

Cramer, R.E., McMaster, M.R., Bartell, P.A. and Dragna, M. (1988) Subject competence and minimisation of the bystander effect. *Journal of Applied Social Psychology* 18, 1133–1148.

Cumberbatch, G. (1987) *The Portrayal of Violence on British Television*. London: BBC Publications.

Cunningham, M.R. (1979) Weather, mood and helping behaviour: quasi-experiments with the sunshine samaritan. *Journal of Personality and Social Psychology* 37, 1947–1956.

Darley, J.M. and Latané, B. (1968) Bystander intervention in emergencies: diffusion of responsibility. *Journal of Personality and Social Psychology* 8, 377–383.

Diener, E., Fraser, S.C., Beaman, A.L. and Kelem, R.T. (1976) Effects of deindividuation variables on stealing among haloween trick or treaters. *Journal of Personality and Social Psychology* 33, 178–183.

Dollard, J., Doob, L., Miller, N.E., Mowrer, O.H. and Sears, R. (1939) *Frustration and Aggression*. Newhaven, CT: Yale University Press.

Donnerstein, E. and Wilson, D.W. (1976) Effects of noise and perceived control on ongoing and subsequent aggressive behaviour. *Journal of Personality and Social Psychology* 34, 774–781.

Dovidio, J.F., Allen, J.L. and Schroeder, D.A. (1990) Specificity of empathy-induced helping: evidence for altruistic motivation. *Journal of Personality and Social Psychology* 59, 249–260.

Durkin, K. (1985) *Television, Sex Roles and Children*. Milton Keynes: Open University Press.

Eagly, A.H. and Crowley, M. (1986) Gender and helping behaviour: a meta-analytic review of the social psychological literature. *Psychological Bulletin* 100, 283–308.

Elliott, D.S., Huizinga, D. and Ageton, S.S. (1985) *Explaining Delinquency and Drug Use*. Beverly Hills CA: Sage.

Ellis, G.T. and Sekgra, F. (1972) The effect of aggressive cartoons on the behaviour of first-grade children. *Journal of Psychology* 81, 37–43.

Eron, L.D. (1982) Parent–child interaction, television violence and aggression in children. *American Psychologist* 37, 197–211.

Eron, L.D., Huesmann, L.R., Brice, P., Fischer, P. and Mermelstein, R. (1983) Age trends in the development of aggression, sex-typing, and related television habits. *Developmental Psychology* 19, 71–77.

Evans, G.W. and Cohen, S. (1987) Environmental stress. In D. Stokols and I. Altman (eds) *Handbook of Environmental Psychology*. New York: Wiley.

Evans, G.W., Palsane, M.N. and Carrere, S. (1987) Type A behaviour and occupational stress: a cross-cultural study of blue-collar workers. *Journal of Personality and Social Psychology* 52, 1002–1007.

Farrington, D.P. (1989) Early predictors of adolescent aggression and adult violence. *Violence and Victims* 4, 79–100.

Feldman, R.E. (1968) Response to compatriot and foreigner who seek assistance. *Journal of Personality and Social Psychology* 10, 202–214.

Felson, R.B. (1978) Aggression as impression management. *Social Psychology* 41, 205–213.

Forge, K.L. and Phemister, S. (1987) The effect of prosocial cartoons on preschool children. *Child Study Journal* 17, 83–88.

Freud, S. (1933) New introductory lectures on psycho-analysis. New York: Norton.

Friedman, M. and Rosenman, R.H. (1974) *Type A Behaviour and Your Heart*. New York: Knopf.

Frodi, A. (1975) The effect of exposure to weapons on aggressive behaviour from a cross-cultural perspective. *International Journal of Psychology* 10, 283–292.

Gaertner, S.L. and Dovidio, J.F. (1977) The subtlety of white racism, arousal and helping behaviour. *Journal of Personality and Social Psychology* 35, 691–707.

Geen, R.G. (1978) Some effects of observing violence upon the behaviour of the observer. In B.A. Maher (ed.), *Progress in Experimental Personality Research* (vol. 8) New York: Academic Press.

Geen, R.G. and O'Neal, E.C. (1969) Activation of cue-eliciting aggression by general arousal. *Journal of Personality and Social Psychology* 11, 289–292.

Geller, E.S. (1988) A behavioural science approach to transport safety. *Bulletin of the New York Academy of Medicine* 64(7), 632–661.

Gerbner, G., Gross, L., Morgan, M. and Signorielli, N. (1980) The Mainstreaming of America. Violence profile no 11. *Journal of Communication* 30, 10–29.

Gergen, K.J., Ellsworth, P. Maslach, C. and Siepel, M. (1975) Obligation, donor resources, and reactions to aid in three cultures. *Journal of Personality and Social Psychology* 31, 390–400.

Gladue, B.A. (1991) Aggressive behavioural characteristics, hormones and sexual orientation in men and women. *Aggressive Behaviour* 17, 313–326.

Goldstein, J. and Arms, R. (1971) Effects of observing athletic contests on hostility. *Sociometry* 54, 83–91.

Gouldner, A.W. (1960) The notion of reciprocity: a preliminary statement. *American Sociological Review* 25, 161–178.

Greenberg, L. (1979) Genetic component of bee odour in kin recognition. *Science* 206, 1095–1097.

Green, F.P. and Schneider, F.W. (1974) Age differences in the behaviour of boys on three measures of altruism. *Child Development* 45, 248–251.

Gunter, B. and McAleer, J.L. (1990) *Children and Television: The One-Eyed monster?* London: Routledge.

Harris, M. (1974) Mediators between frustration and aggression in a field experiment. *Journal of Experimental and Social Psychology* 10, 561–571.

Hartshorne, H. and May, M.A. (1929) *Studies in the Nature of Character: Studies in Service and Self Control* (vol. 2). New York: Macmillan.

Hennigan, K.M., Heath, L., Wharton, J.D., Del Rosario, M.L., Cook, T.D. and Calder, B.J. (1982) Impact of the introduction of television on crime in the United States: empirical findings and theoretical implications. *Journal of Personality and Social Psychology* 42, 461–477.

Hewstone, M. (1988) *Introduction to Social Psychology*. Oxford: Blackwell.

Hoffman (1981) Is altruism a part of human nature? *Journal of Personality and Social Psychology* 40, 121–137.

Homans, G.C. (1961) *Social Behaviour: Its elementary forms*. New York: Harcourt Brace Jovanovich.

Howard, J.L., Liptzin, M.B. and Reifler, C.B. (1973) Is pornography a problem? *Journal of Social Issues* 29(3): 133–145.

Huesmann, L.R. (1988) An information processing model for the development of aggression. *Aggressive Behaviour* 14, 13–24.

Huesmann, L.R., Eron, L.D., Lefkowitz, M.M. and Walder, L.O. (1988) Stability of aggression over time and generations. *Developmental Psychology* 20, 1120–1134.

Hull, J.G. and Bond, C.F. (1986) Social and behavioural consequences of alcohol consumption and expectatancy: a meta-analysis. *Psychological Bulletin* 99, 347–360.

Huston, T.L., Ruggiero, M. Conner, R. and Geis, G. (1981) Bystander intervention into crime: a study based on naturally-occurring episodes. *Social Psychology Quarterly* 44(1), 14–23.

Isen, A.M. (1984) Toward understanding the role of affect in cognition. In R.S. Wyer and T.K. Krull (eds), *Handbook of Social Cognition*. Hillsdale, NJ: Erlbaum.

Isen, A.M. and Levin, P.F. (1972) The effect of feeling good on helping: cookies and kindness. *Journal of Personality and Social Psychology* 21, 384–388.

Jaffe, Y., Feingold, J. and Feohbach, S. (1974) Sexual arousal and behavioural aggression. *Journal of Personality and Social Psychology* 30, 759–764.

Jorgensen, D.O. and Dukes, F.O. (1976) Deindividuation as a function of density and group membership. *Journal of Personality and Social Psychology* 34, 24–39.

Josephson, W.D. (1987) Television violence and children's aggression: testing the priming, social script, and dis-inhibition prediction. *Journal of Personality and Social Psychology* 53, 759–764.

Konner, M. (1982) *The Tangled Wing*. New York: HRW.

Kulik, J. and Brown, R. (1979) Frustration, attribution of blame and aggression. *Journal of Experimental Social Psychology* 15, 183–194.

Latané, B. and Dabbs, J.M. (1975) Sex, group size and helping in three cities. *Sociometry* 38, 108–194.

Latané, B. and Darley, J.M. (1970) *The Unresponsive Bystander: Why Doesn't He Help?* New York: Appleton Century Crofts.

Latané, B. and Darley, J.M. (1976) Help in a crisis: bystander response in an emergency. In J.W. Thibaut and J.T. Spence (eds), *Contemporary Topics in Social Psychology*. Morristown, NJ: General Learning Press.

Lefkowitz, M.M., Eron, L.D., Walder, L.D. and Huesmann, L.R (1977) *Growing Up to be Violent: A Longitudinal Study of the Development of Aggression*. New York: Pergamon Press.

Lerner, M.J. (1970) The desire for justice and reactions to victims. In J. Macaulay and L. Bewrkowitz (eds), *Altruism and Helping Behaviour*. New York: Academic Press.

Lerner, M.J. (1975) The justice motive in social behaviour. *Journal of Social Issues* 31(3), 1–19.

Levine, R.V., Martinez, T.S., Brase, G and Sorenson, K. (1994) Helping in 36 US cities. *Journal of Personality and Social Psychology* 67, 69–82.

Leyens, J.P., Camino, L., Parke, R.D. and Berkowitz, L. (1975) Effects of movie violence on aggression in a field setting as a function of group dominance and cohesion. *Journal of Personality and Social Psychology* 32, 346–360.

Liebert, R.M. and Baron, R.A. (1972) Some immediate effects of televised violence on children's behaviour. *Developmental Psychology* 6, 469–475.

Lorenz, K. (1966) *On Aggression*. New York: Harcourt, Brace and World.

Magoo, G. and Khanna, R. (1991) Altruism and willingness to donate blood. *Journal of Personality and Clinical Studies* 7, 21–24.

Marsh, P., Rosser, E. and Harre, R. (1978) *The Rules of Disorder*. London: Routledge.

Maruyama, G., Fraser, S.C. and Miller, N. (1982) Personal responsibility and altruism in children. *Journal of Personality and Social Psychology* 42 (4), 658–664.

Mathews, K.E. and Canon, L.K. (1975) Environmental noise level as a determinant of helping behaviour. *Journal of Personality and Social Psychology* 32, 571–577.

Messenger-Davies, M. (1989) *Television is Good for Your Kids*. London: Hilary Shipman Ltd.

Midlarsky, E. and Bryan, J.H. (1967) Training charity in children. *Journal of Personality and Social Psychology* 5, 408–415.

Midlarsky, E., Bryan, J.H. and Brickman, P. (1973) Aversive approval: interactive effects of modelling and reinforcement on altruistic behaviour. *Child Development* 44, 321–328.

Milavsky, J.R., Kessler, R., Stipp, H. and Rubens, W.S. (1982) Television and aggression: results of a panel study. In D. Pearl, L. Bouthilet and J. Lazar (eds), *Television and Behaviour: Ten Years of Scientific Progress and Implications for the Eighties.* National Institute of Mental Health.

Milgram, S. (1963) Behavioural study of obedience. *Journal of Abnormal and Social Psychology* 67, 371–378.

Milgram, S. (1965) Some conditions of obedience and disobedience to authority. *Human Relations* 18, 57–65.

Milgram, S. (1970) The experience of living in cities. *Science* 167, 1461–1468.

Milgram, S., and Shotland, R.L. (1973) *Television and Anti-social Behaviour.* New York: Academic Press.

Mills, R.S.L. and Grusec, J.E. (1989) Cognitive, affective and behavioural consequences of praising altruism. *Merrill-Palmer Quarterly* 35(3), 299–326.

Moghaddam, F.M., Taylor, D.M. and Wright, S.C. (1993*) Social Psychology in Cross-cultural Perspective.* New York: W.H. Freeman.

Moss, M.K. and Page, R.A. (1972) Reinforcement and helping behaviour. *Journal of Applied Social Psychology* 2, 360–371.

Newson, E. (1994) Video violence and the protection of children. *The Psychologist* 7 (6), 272–274.

Nobles, W.W. (1976) Extended self: rethinking the so-called negro self concept. *Journal of Black Psychology* 2(2), 15–24.

Ohbuchi, K., Kamdea, M. and Agarie, N. (1989) Apology as aggression control: its role in mediating appraisal of and response to harm. *Journal of Personality and Social Psychology* 56, 219–227.

Olweus, D. (1979) Stability of aggressive reaction patterns in males: a review. *Psychological Bulletin* 86, 852–875.

Osterwell, Z. and Nagano-Nakamura, K. (1992) Maternal views on aggression: Japan and Israel. *Aggressive Behaviour* 18, 263–270.

Page, M.P. and Scheidt, A.H. (1971) The elusive weapons effect: demand awareness, evaluation apprehension and slightly sophisticated subjects. *Journal of Personality and Social Psychology* 20, 304–318.

Page, R.A. (1977) Noise and helping behaviour. *Environment and Behaviour* 9, 559–572.

Page, R.A. (1978) Environmental influences on prosocial behaviour: the effect of temperature. Paper presented at Midwestern Psychological Association meeting.

Pancer, S.M., McMullen, L.M., Kabatoff, R.A., Johnson, K.G. and Pond, C.A. (1979) Conflict and avoidance in helping situations. *Journal of Personality and Social Psychology* 37, 1406–1411.

Parke, R.D., Berkowitz, L. Leyens, J.P., West, S.G. and Sebastian, R.J. (1977) Some effects of violent and nonviolent movies on the behaviour of juvenile delinquents. In l. Berkowitz (ed.), 1977 *Advances in Experimental Social Psychology* (vol. 10). New York: Academic Press.

Patterson, G.R. (1980) Mothers: the unacknowledged victims. Monographs for the Society for Research. *Child Development* 45, 5, 18b.

Piliavin, J.A., Dovidio, J.F., Gaertner, S.L. and Clark, R.D. (1981) *Emergency Intervention*. New York: Academic Press.

Piliavin, J.M., Rodin, J. and Piliavin, J.A. (1969) Good Samaritanism: an underground phenomenon? *Journal of Personality and Social Psychology* 13(4), 289–299.

Pomazal, R.J. and Clore, G.L. (1973) Helping on the highway: the effects of dependency and sex. *Journal of Applied Social Psychology* 3, 150–164.

Prentice-Dunn, S. and Rogers, R.W. (1983) Deindividuation in aggression. In R.G. Green and E.I. Donnerstein (eds), *Aggression: Theoretical and Empirical Reviews*. New York: Academic Press.

Przybyla, D.P.J. (1985) The facilitating effects of exposure to erotica on male pro-social behaviour. PhD thesis, State University of New York in Albany, NY.

Regan, D.T. (1968) The effects of favour and liking on compliance. Unpublished doctoral dissertation, Stanford University.

Reicher, S.D. (1984a) Social influence in the crowd: attitudinal and behavioural effects of deindividuation in conditions of high and low group salience. *British Journal of Social Psychology* 23, 341–350.

Reicher, S.D. (1984b) The St Paul's riot: an explanation of the limits of crowd action in terms of a social identity model. *European Journal of Social Psychology* 14, 1–21.

Rheingold, H.L. (1982) Little children's participation in the work of adults: a nascent pro-social behaviour. *Child Development* 53, 114–125.

Rosenthal, A.M. (1964) *Thirty-Eight Witnesses*. New York: McGraw-Hill.

Rotton, J., Frey, J., Barry, T., Milligan, M. and Fitzpatrick, M. (1979) The air pollution experience and interpersonal aggression. *Journal of Applied Social Psychology* 9, 397–412.

Rushton, J.P. (1975) Generosity in children: immediate and long term effects of modelling, preaching and moral judgement. *Journal of Personality and Social Psychology* 31, 459–466.

Rushton, J.P. (1989) Genetic similarity, mate choice, and fecundity in humans. *Ethology and Sociobiology* 9, 329–333.

Samerotte, G.C. and Harris, M.B. (1976) Some factors influencing helping: the effects of handicap, responsibility and requesting help. *Journal of Social Psychology* 98, 39–45.

Schneider, F.W., Lesko, W.A. and Garrett, W.A. (1980) Helping behaviour in hot, uncomfortable and cold temperatures. *Environment and Behaviour* 12, 231–240.

Schutte, N.S., Malouff, J.M., Post-Gorden, J.C. and Rodasts, A.L. (1988) Effect of playing videogames on children's aggressive and other behaviour. *Journal of Applied Social Psychology* 18, 454–460.

Schwartz, S. (1977) Normative influences on altruism. In l. Berkowitz (ed.) (1977) *Advances in Experimental Social Psychology* (vol. 10). New York: Academic Press.

Sears, R.R., Maccoby, E. and Levine, H. (1957) *Patterns of Child Rearing*. Evanston, IL: Row Peterson.

Shaffer, D. (1985) *Developmental Psychology*. Monterey, CA: Brooks/Cole.

Shotland, R.L. and Huston, T.L. (1979) Emergencies: what are they and do they influence bystanders to intervene? *Journal of Personality and Social Psychology* 37(10), 1822–1834.

Shotland, R.L. and Straw, M.K. (1976) Bystander response to an assault: when a man attacks a woman. *Journal of Personality and Social Psychology* 34, 990–999.

Smith, K.D., Keating, J.P. and Stotland, E. (1989) Altruism reconsidered: the effect of denying feedback on a victim's status to empathetic witnesses. *Journal of Personality and Social Psychology* 57, 641–650.

Sprafkin, J.N. and Rubinstein, E.A. (1979) A field correlational study of children's television viewing habits and pro-social behaviour. *Journal of Broadcasting* 23, 265–276.

Sprafkin, J.N., Liebert, R.M. and Poulos, R.W. (1975) Effects of pro-social televised example on children's helping. *Journal of Experimental Child Psychology* 20, 119–126.

Staub, E. (1979) *Positive Social Behaviour and Morality* (vol. 2). New York: Academic Press.

Steele, C.M. and Southwick, L. (1985) Alcohol and social behaviour I: the psychology of drunken excess. *Journal of Personality and Social Psychology* 48, 18–34.

Stein, A.H. and Friedrich, L.K. (1972) Television content and young children's behaviour. In J.P. Murray, E.A. Rubinstein and G.A. Comstock (eds), *Television and Social Behaviour, Vol. 2: Television and Social Learning.* Washington, DC: US Government Printing Office.

Strube, M., Turner, C.W., Cerro, D., Stevens, J. and Hinchey, F. (1984) Interpersonal aggression and the type A coronary-prone behaviour pattern: a theoretical distinction and practical implications. *Journal of Personality and Social Psychology* 47, 839–847.

Taylor, S.P. and Gammon, C.B. (1976) Aggressive behaviour of intoxicated subjects: the effect of third-party intervention. *Journal of Studies on Alcohol* 34, 938–941.

Taylor, S.P. and Sears, J.D. (1988) The effects of alcohol and persuasive social pressure on human physical aggression. *Aggressive Behaviour* 14, 237–243.

Toch, H. (1980) *Violent Men.* Cambridge, MA: Schenkman.

Triandis, H.C. (1994) *Culture and Social Behaviour.* New York: McGraw-Hill.

Trivers, R.L. (1971) The evolution of reciprocal altruism. *Quarterly Review of Biology* 46, 35–57.

Turnbull, C.M. (1972) *The Mountain People.* New York: Simon & Schuster.

Walster, E. and Piliavin, J.A. (1972) Equity and the innocent bystander. *Journal of Social Issues* 28(3), 165–189.

Watson, R.I. (1973) Investigation into deindividuation using a cross-cultural survey technique. *Journal of Personality and Social Psychology* 25, 342–345.

West, S.G. and Brown, T.J. (1975) Physical attractiveness, the severity of the emergency and helping. *Journal of Experimental Social Psychology* 11, 531–538.

Whiting, B.B. and Whiting, J.W.M. (1975) *Children of Six Cultures.* Cambridge, MA: Harvard University Press.

Williams, T.M. (1986) *The Impact of Television: A Natural Experiment Involving Three Towns.* New York: Academic Press.

Wilson, E.O. (1975) *Sociobiology, the New Synthesis.* Cambridge, MA: Harvard University Press.

Wright, P.M., George, J.M., Farnsworth, R.N. and McMahan, G.C. (1993) Productivity and extra role behaviour: the effects of goals and incentives on spontaneous helping. *Journal of Applied Psychology* 78, 374–381.

Zillmann, D. (1988) Cognition-excitation interdependencies in aggressive behaviour. *Aggressive Behaviour* 14, 51–64.

Zillmann, D., Katcher, A.H. and Milavsky, B. (1972) Excitation transfer from physical exercise to subsequent aggressive behaviour. *Journal of Experimental Social Psychology* 8, 247–259.

Zillmann, D. and Bryant, J. (1974) Effect of residual excitation on the emotional response to provocation and delayed aggressive behaviour. *Journal of Personality and Social Psychology* 30, 782–791.

Zimbardo, P.G. (1969) The human choice: individuation, reason and order versus deindividuation, impulse and chaos. In W.J. Arnold and D. Levine (eds), *Nebraska Symposium on Motivation* (vol. 17). University of Nebraska Press.

Index